Englisch
Übungen und Tests

von Willy Piert

Ernst Klett Stuttgart

Herausgegeben von
Willy Piert, Studiendirektor und Dozent an der Volkshochschule Köln,
unter Mitwirkung der Verlagsredaktion Neue Sprachen.
Mitarbeit an diesem Buch:
Wolfgang H. Kaul, M. A., Redaktionsleiter; Derrick Jenkins, Verlagsredakteur.

1. Auflage 1 9 8 7 6 | 1985 84 83 82

Alle Drucke dieser Auflage können im Unterricht nebeneinander benutzt werden. Die letzte Zahl bezeichnet das Jahr dieses Druckes.

Einbandgestaltung: H. Köhler, Stuttgart
Druck: Eckstein + Stähle, Stuttgart. Printed in Germany.
ISBN 3-12-504650-5 – Ernst Klett, Stuttgart.

Inhalt

Lektion		Seite
1	A Visit	4
2	A Stationer's Shop	5
3	An Evening Out	7
4	The Red Paint	9
5	Spoilt Holidays	11
6	Red Riding Hood and the Wolf	13
7	A Letter	15
8	Charlie's New Home	17
9	The Big Store	20
10	At the Marriage Agency	22
	Test I	24
11	A Week at the Seaside	28
12	Christmas in England	30
13	Landing at Dover	31
14	The Ideal Husband	34
	Revision Exercises I	36
15	Under the Roofs of London	39
16	He Says It the English Way	41
17	Betting, a National Amusement	44
18	A Ticket to Washington	46
19	A Sunday in Hyde Park	48
20	Teaching English	50
	Test II	53
21	Alone Among Millions	56
22	Safety Last	58
23	Friday the Thirteenth	60
24	A Murder has been Planned	62
25	The Proof	64
26	The Man who was Waiting for his Wife	67
27	Journey's End	70
28	The World Food Crisis	72
	Revision Exercises II	74
29	The Problem of Automation	78
30	The Open Window	79
31	Don't	81
32	Stratford-on-Avon	83
33	Starting a New Life in Australia	86
	Test III	88
34	The Boat Race	91
35	Sales Psychology	93
36	For Whites Only? I	96
37	For Whites Only? II	99
38	London Through the Ages	101
39	The Channel Tunnel	104
40	North Sea Gas and Oil	105
41	From Empire to Commonwealth I	107
42	From Empire to Commonwealth II	109
	Test IV	110
	Revision Exercises III	117
	Schlüssel zu den Tests	121

1 A Visit

1. Setze die Wörter sinngemäß ein (Fill in the right words)

actor, better (2×), egg, fetch, finished, hand, hat, ill, kiss, sister, tea

Mrs Sim: "(1) ... Mr Dent in, Ann." Mr Dent is an (2) ... Mr Dent and Mrs Sim have (3) ... Mrs Sim says: "(4) ... me cheese and biscuits, please." Mrs Sim has cheese, Mr Dent has an (5) ... Mrs Sim says: "Ken is (6) ... in bed." – "Is he (7) ...?" – "Yes, he is (8) ..." Tea is (9) ... Mr Dent gets his (10) ... He gives Mrs Sim a (11) ... Mrs Sim is Mr Dent's (12) ...

2. Was sie einander sagen

1. Mr Dent says to Ann: "Is Mrs ...?" 2. Ann says to Mr Dent: "Yes, ... " 3. Ann says to Mrs Sim: "It ..." 4. Mrs Sim says to Ann: "Fetch ..." 5. Mrs Sim says to Mr Kent: "Ken ..." 6. Mr Dent says to Mrs Sim: "Is ..." 7. Mrs Sim says to Ann: "Give ..." 8. Ann says to Mrs Sim: "And ...?"

3. Mr Dent has, Mr and Mrs Sim have

Setze in der 3. Person Einzahl *has,* in der 3. Person Mehrzahl *have* ein

1. Mr Dent ... an egg. 2. Mr Dent and his sister ... tea. 3. Ann and Mrs Sim ... biscuits. 4. Mr Sim ... cheese.

4. Lies und setze in die Schriftsprache um

1. iz mistə ˈdent‿ən‿ˈæktə? 2. jes, mistə ˈdent‿ˈiz‿ən‿ˈæktə. 3. iz misiz‿ˈsim mistə ˈdents‿ˈsistə? 4. jes, misiz‿ˈsim‿iz mistə ˈdents‿ˈsistə. 5. iz mistə ˈsim‿ˈil? 6. jes, mistə ˈsim‿iz‿ˈil. 7. iz hi:‿in ˈbed? 8. jes, mistə ˈsim‿iz‿in ˈbed. 9. iz hi: ˈbetə? 10. jes, hi:z ˈbetə.

5. Setze in die Schriftsprache um

Beispiel: mistə ˈdents ˈhæt = Mr Dent's hat

1. mistə ˈsimz ˈbed 2. ænz‿ˈeg 3. kenz ˈti: 4. misiz‿ˈsimz ˈbiskits 5. ən‿ˈæktəz hæt 6. ə ˈsistəz ˈkis

6. Übersetze

1. Herr Dent ist ein Schauspieler. 2. Er sagt: „Anna, ist Frau Sim zu Hause?“ 3. Anna sagt: „Ja, Herr Dent, Frau Sim ist zu Hause.“ 4. Frau Sim und Herr Dent trinken Tee. 5. Herr Sim ist krank. 6. Er ist im Bett. 7. Frau Sim sagt zu Anna: „Bitte geben Sie Herrn Sim seinen Tee und ein Ei. 8. Es geht ihm besser.“ 9. Die Teestunde ist vorbei. 10. Frau Sim sagt: „Anna, holen Sie Herrn Dents Hut.“ 11. Herr Dent gibt Frau Sim einen Kuß. 12. Frau Sim ist seine Schwester.

2 A Stationer's Shop

1. Fill in the right words

assistant, boss (2×), buy, enters, entertaining, expensive, leaves, opposite, pictures, stationer's, takes, thanks, typist, wants

Tom is an (1) … in a shop. It is a (2) … shop. Who is the (3) …? Mr Smith is the (4) … Betty White (5) … the shop. She is a (6) … in an office. The office is (7) … the shop. Miss White (8) … a newspaper. Mr Smith says: “(9) … *The Daily Mail.* This paper has nice (10) … and (11) … articles.” Miss White (12) … *The Daily Mail.* It is not (13) … “Many (14) …, Miss White.” She (15) … the shop.

2. Setze in die Mehrzahl

Beispiel (Example): This is a *shop. – These* are *shops.*

1. newspaper 2. pen 3. pencil 4. postcard 5. shop 6. sweet 7. picture 8. entertaining article 9. assistant 10. expensive pen

3. is oder are ?

1. Mr Dent … an actor. 2. He … in Mr Smith's shop. 3. Tom … an assistant in the shop. 4. Mr Dent says: “These … nice pens, Tom. 5. … these pens expensive?” 6. “These pens … not expensive, Mr Dent. 7. The pencils … expensive.” 8. Miss White enters the shop. “Who … this nice little thing, Tom?” 9. “This … Miss White. 10. She … a typist in the office opposite.” 11. Miss White wants a paper.

She opens the paper. Mr Dent's picture ... in the paper. 12. Miss White says: "This ... a nice picture, Tom. 13. Who ... these two actors?" 14. "The actors ... Mr Dent and Mr Sim." 15. Miss White says: "Mr Dent ... sweet." She takes the paper. Mr Dent says: "Many thanks, Miss White." He gives Miss White his picture.

4. Lies

1. The actor in the picture is Mr Dent. 2. The assistant in the shop is not the boss. 3. The nice pens are expensive. 4. The expensive pencils are better. 5. The pictures are entertaining. 6. The shop is opposite the office. 7. The entertaining pictures are not in the Times.

5. Ordne die Wörter nach den Lauten [ai], [ei], [əu], [ð], [θ]

Beispiel (Example): [ai] good-b**ye**

1. aw**ay** 2. d**ai**ly 3. entert**ai**ning 4. g**o** 5. good-b**ye** 6. kn**ow** 7. **o**pen 8. p**a**per 9. p**o**st-card 10. sh**ow** 11. Smi**th** 12. **th**anks 13. **th**e two papers 14. **th**ing 15. **th**is 16. **th**ese 17. wh**i**te

6. Übersetze

Der tägliche Besuch

1. Wer betritt das Schreibwarengeschäft? 2. Anna betritt den Laden. 3. Tom, der Verkäufer, sagt: „Der tägliche Besuch! 4. Herr Sim möchte die *Times,* Frau Sim die *Daily Mail.*“ 5. Anna sagt: „Der Chef ist krank. 6. Er liegt im Bett. 7. Es geht ihm besser. 8. Er möchte den *Guardian.*“ 9. Tom sagt: „Ich kenne Herrn Sim und seine Politik! Was für ein Unsinn! 10. (Er öffnet eine Zeitung.) Die *Daily Mail* ist unterhaltend, Anna. 11. (Er zeigt die Bilder.) Dies ist Herrn Dents Hochzeit. 12. Nehmen Sie ein Bonbon, Anna.“ 13. Toms Chef betritt den Laden. 14. Anna sagt: „Auf Wiedersehen, Tom.“ 15. Sie verläßt den Laden.

3 An Evening Out

1. Fill in the right words

bus, cinema, fine, free, full, good, here, instead, last, mind, pictures, pockets, rush hour, sorry, taxi, theatres, time

Bill has (1) … tickets for the Empire. That is a big (2) … "What about the (3) …, Sally?" – "That's (4) …, Bill. Let's take a (5) …" – "Why not a (6) …? We have plenty of (7) …" The streets are (8) … of cars. It is the (9) … Piccadilly at (10) … Lights, (11) …, cinemas. "(12) … we are," says Bill.
The man looks at the tickets, but he says: "(13) …, these are bus tickets. They are no (14) …" Bill looks in his (15) … He says: "I'm sorry, Sally." – "Never (16) …, darling. Let's have a drink (17) …"

2. Beantworte die Fragen mit 'he, she, it' usw.

Example: Why is Mr Sim in bed? (ill)
He is ill.

1. Why has Mrs Sim a kiss for Mr Dent? (sister) 2. Why is *The Daily Mail* an entertaining paper? (plenty of pictures) 3. Why are the streets full of cars? (rush hour) 4. Why are Bill's tickets no good? (bus tickets)

3. Setze die entsprechenden Formen von 'to be' und 'to have' ein

Bill: The cinema (1) … full. (2) … you sad Sally?

Sally: No, Bill, I (3) … not. 'The Green Monster' (4) … not an entertaining film. The actors (5) … no good. The tickets (6) … expensive. A nice drink (7) … better.

Bill: I (8) … tickets for the theatre.

Sally: What (9) … on, Bill?

Bill: 'Piccadilly's Nice Little Things'. The actors (10) … good. Mr Dent (11) … in it.

Sally: (12) … we plenty of time, Bill?

Bill: Yes, we (13) …

Sally: Fine. Let's (14) … a drink.

4. Setze die entsprechenden Formen des persönlichen Fürworts ein

1. Miss White enters the stationer's shop. ... is a typist. 2. ... is a nice little thing. 3. Tom is in the shop. ... is an assistant. 4. What is in the shop? ... sells newspapers, pens, pencils, sweets and tobacco. 5. Miss White says: "... want an entertaining newspaper. 6. Have ... an entertaining newspaper, Mr Smith?" 7. Mr Smith says: "Oh yes, Miss White. ... have plenty of entertaining papers." 8. ... shows *The Times* and *The Guardian.* 9. Miss White says: "These papers are full of politics, Mr Smith. ... aren't entertaining. 10. ... want a paper full of pictures."

5. Übersetze

Ein Ausgehabend für Anna

1. Herr Sim ist nicht in seinem Büro. 2. Er liegt im Bett. 3. Frau Sim hat Karten fürs Theater. 4. Sie ist traurig. 5. Herr Sim ist krank. 6. Frau Sim sagt: „Macht nichts! Es ist nicht nett im West End. 7. Die Straßen sind voller Autos. 8. Die Taxen sind teuer. 9. Wie wär's mit Anna?" 10. Herr Sim sagt: „Ja, gib Anna die Karten." 11. Der Abend ist unterhaltend für Anna.

6. Übersetze

Das Grüne Licht

1. Fräulein White ist im Schreibwarengeschäft. 2. Tom sagt: „Wie wär's mit dem Kino, Betty? 3. Ich habe Karten für ‚Das grüne Licht'. 4. Ich habe einen Wagen. 5. Der Film beginnt in zehn Minuten. 6. Gehen wir (= Laß uns gehen)." 7. Es ist Hauptverkehrszeit. 8. Ampeln an jeder Kreuzung! 9. Tom sagt am Kinoeingang: „Es tut mir leid, Betty. Ich kann die Karten nicht finden." 10. Betty sagt: „Macht nichts, Tom. 11. Ich kenne den Film. Er ist nicht unterhaltend." 12. Tom sagt: „Hier ist ein Bonbon, Betty. 13. Süßigkeiten für die Süße *(sweet)*." 14. Der Abend ist nicht teuer für Tom.

4 The Red Paint

1. Fill in the right words

answer, bathroom, bathrooms, black, brush, colour, cries, door, downstairs, garden, house, idea, thinks, upstairs, where

Mr and Mrs Brown have a small (1) … in Wimbledon. Mr Brown is (2) … in the sitting-room. (3) … is Mrs Brown? She is in the (4) … Mr Brown gets an (5) … He (6) …: "I have a (7) … and red paint. There are plenty of white (8) …, but how many houses have a red (9) …?"
He goes (10) … and begins to paint. Mrs Brown knocks at the (11) … There is no (12) … She enters and (13) …: "What's this? What an awful (14) …!"
Mr Brown: "This is a (15) … day for my red bath."

2. Setze in die Mehrzahl (Use the plural)

a) *Example:* There's a pink flower in the garden.
There are pink flowers in the garden.

1. There's a car at the crossing. 2. There's a biscuit on the floor. 3. There's a ticket for 'The Green Monster' in my pocket. 4. There's a taxi in the street. 5. There's a blue chair in the sitting-room.

b) *Verwandle die Sätze in Fragen und verneine*
Example: Is there a pink flower in the garden? No, there isn't.

c) *Setze die Sätze von b) in die Mehrzahl*
Example: Are there pink flowers in the garden? No, there aren't.

3. Use the plural: 'These – Those'

Example: This is a white house and that is a red house.
These are white houses and *those* are red houses.

1. This bus ticket is pink and that cinema ticket is yellow. 2. This egg is white and that egg is brown. 3. This shoe is green and that shoe is blue. 4. This bath is black and that bath is red. 5. This hat is pink and that hat is grey. 6. This blue book is interesting, that red book is not interesting.

4. Fill in 'what – why – how many'

Example: ... colour is the window frame?
What colour is the window frame?

1. ... about a drink? 2. ... houses have red bathrooms? 3. ... colour is Mrs Brown's hair? 4. ... is Mrs Brown sad? 5. ... is Mr Brown's motto? 6. ... is Mr Brown sorry?

5. Ordne nach den Lauten

a) [ɛə], [ɑ:], [ɔ:], [ʌ], [au]

1. about 2. answer 3. article 4. awful 5. bath 6. boring 7. brown 8. brush 9. bus 10. car 11. chair 12. colour 13. door 14., 15. downstairs (2×) 16. floor 17. for 18. garden 19. how 20. at last 21. out 22., 23. rush hour (2×) 24. there 25., 26. upstairs (2×) 27. where

b) [ə], [æ], [e], [ɔ]

1., 2. actor (2×) 3. assistant 4. bed 5., 6. better (2×) 7. boss 8. egg 9., 10. entertaining (2×) 11. expensive 12. to fetch 13. to get 14. to hand 15. to have 16. he has 17. hat 18. many 19., 20. nonsense (2×) 21. office 22., 23. opposite (2×) 24. paper 25. picture 26. sad 27. he says 28. sorry

c) [s], [z], [v], [w]

1. what 2., 3. expensive (2×) 4. he enters 5. he gets 6., 7. he says (2×) 8., 9. pencils (2×) 10. pens 11. pictures 12. shoes 13. where 14., 15. she gives (2×) 16., 17. she sells (2×) 18. The Times 19. why 20., 21. visit (2×) 22., 23. she wants (2×)

6. ich mag, ich habe gern, mir gefällt = 'I like'

Example: Dieser Mann gefällt mir. – I like this man.

1. Ich mag Tee und süße Kekse. 2. Ich habe Blumen gern. 3. Mir gefallen rote Wagen. 4. Die gelben Blumen dort gefallen meiner Schwester. 5. Die Bilder in dieser Zeitung gefallen Herrn und Frau Brown. 6. Rotes Haar gefällt mir. 7. Er mag hübsche Bilder. 8. Ihm gefällt der Wahlspruch: „Trautes Heim, Glück allein!" *(Home, sweet home)*

7. Übersetze (Translate)

1. Was ist in deiner Tasche? 2. Welche Farbe hat dein Wagen? 3. Wieviele Taxis gibt es in London? 4. Wieviele Zimmer gibt es in Herrn Browns Haus? 5. Wer hat eine gute Idee? 6. Wer gibt dem Schauspieler Blumen? 7. Warum sind diese Blumen teuer?

5 Spoilt Holidays

1. Fill in the right words

before, body, comes, enjoys, fills, hard, headache, health, hot, husband, in (2×), measles, on, shock, shuts, spots, tired, towel

It is two days (1) … Mr Turner's holidays. He (2) … home from the office. He is very (3) … and he has a (4) … Mrs Turner says: "Take a (5) … bath. It's good for your (6) …" Mr Turner goes upstairs to the bathroom. He turns (7) … the water. The water (8) … the bath. He gets (9) … Mr Turner (10) … his eyes. He (11) … the warmth. Now Mr Turner opens his eyes. He gets a (12) … His (13) … is covered with red (14) … He takes a (15) … and rubs (16) … Mrs Turner comes (17) … She sees her (18) … She says: "Oh John, you have German (19) …"

2. Setze das besitzanzeigende Fürwort ein

Example: Bill and Sally are in … sitting-room.
Bill and Sally are in *their* sitting-room.

Bill: Where is (1) … brush?

Sally: (2) … brush is in the bathroom. Take off (3) … jacket, (4) … pullover, (5) … tie and (6) … shirt when you paint.

Bill: Where is the paint?

Sally: The paint is in (7) … car. But why paint this evening?

Bill: I like (8) … hobby. And you? (9) … hobby is (10) … garden.

Sally: (11) … garden is beautiful, (12) … paint is awful. What about TV this evening?

Bill: What's on?

Sally: 'Home, sweet home!' It's an entertaining film.

Bill: You and (13) … entertaining films! They are boring.

Sally: You and (14) ... paint! You're boring, too. You aren't very interesting. *(Bill shuts* (15) ... *eyes, but says nothing.)* You are an awful man. (16) ... evening is spoilt. *(Bill opens his eyes. He looks at his wife and* (17) ... *red face.)*

Bill: No, Sally, (18) ... evening isn't spoilt. Let's go and see Betty Dent in (19) ... film 'Black is the Colour'. I've tickets for the cinema.

3. Lies (Read)

a) [st – sp]: The stationer's shop is downstairs. Upstairs there is no bathroom. There's a sitting-room instead. There are some spots on the walls, and the room is spoilt.
b) [r]: Sorry, the Greens aren't very interesting. All three are very boring, but I go there for free drinks.
c) [v – w]: A visit to the West End is very, very expensive. Let's have an evening at home with TV, whisky and water.

4. Ordne nach den Lauten [ə:], [dʒ], [tʃ]

1. **ch**air 2. **ch**eese 3. **ch**est 4. to fe**tch** 5. **j**acket 6. **j**ust 7., 8. **Ger**man (2 ×) 9. **J**ohn 10. pic**tu**re 11. sh**ir**t 12. to t**ur**n 13. T**ur**ner 14. h**er** eyes 15. to **j**ump

5. Translate

"Home, Sweet Home"

3 4 5 1 2

1. Herr Brown kommt von seinem Laden nach Hause. 2. Er geht nach oben. 3. Er möchte ein Bad. 4. Er dreht das Wasser auf. 5. Herr Brown zieht seine Krawatte, sein Hemd, die Schuhe, die Socken, die Hose aus. 6. Er steigt hinein. Das Wasser ist gerade recht. 7. Herr Brown schließt die (!) Augen. 8. Er genießt sein Bad. 9. Er nimmt die Abendzeitung. 10. Er öffnet die Zeitung und schaut die Bilder an. 11. Die Zeitung ist interessant heute: „Verdorbene Ferien für Herrn Dent, den Schauspieler. 12. Er hat [die] Röteln.“ 13. „Ein schwarzer Tag für Londons West-End-Verkehr!“ 14. „Das Fernsehprogramm ist schrecklich!“ 15. Ein Bad mit einer Zeitung, welch ein Vergnügen! 16. Frau Brown klopft an die Tür. 17. Es kommt keine Antwort. 18. Sie denkt: „Ist John krank?“ 19. Sie tritt ein und sieht ihren Mann mit der Zeitung im Bad. 20. Sie sagt: „Komm nach unten! Laß uns Tee trinken. Hier ist dein Handtuch.“ 21. Herr Brown sagt nichts, aber er denkt: „Trautes Heim, Glück allein.“

6 Red Riding Hood and the Wolf

1. Fill in the right words

at, away, back, basket, doing, dress, for, gone, lot, mirror, near, number, out, round, shoes, starts, stop, stops, way

Betsy is standing in front of the (1) … What is she (2) …? She is putting on her red (3) …, her red cap, her best stockings and red (4) … Her mother says: "Go and see Grandma, Betsy. Take the (5) … eleven bus. Here is a (6) … with cake and fruit in it." A (7) … of people are waiting (8) … the bus stop. A young man asks: "Are you waiting (9) … a bus? Let's take my car." They go (10) … the corner and get in. The car (11) … Betsy says: "My grandma lives (12) … Hyde Park. This is not the (13) … to Hyde Park. Please (14) … the car."

There is a red traffic light. The car (15) … Betsy jumps (16) … and runs (17) … – But where is the basket for Grandma? Betsy runs (18) … The car is (19) …

2. Say what the people are doing

Setze die Verlaufsform ein

a) *The pictures in Lesson 1*

Example: Mrs Sim and Mr Dent (to have) tea
Mrs Sim and Mr Dent *are having* tea.

1. They (to sit) at a table 2. Mr Dent (to have) an egg 3. Mr Sim (to wait) for Ann 4. Ann (to give) Mr Sim his tea and an egg 5. Mr Dent (to say) good-bye to Mrs Sim 6. He (to give) Mrs Sim a kiss

b) *What are the people doing in Lesson 2?*

1. Three people (to stand) in the stationer's shop 2. Mr Smith, the boss, (to stand) in the corner 3. He (to look) at Tom and Betty 4. The assistant (to ask) Betty what she wants

c) *The picture (in front of the cinema) in Lesson 3*

1. Bill and Sally (to stand) in front of the cinema 2. Bill (to look) in his pockets 3. The man at the entrance (to wait) for the tickets 4. The cinema (to show) 'The Green Monster' 5. The lady in the box-office (to sell) tickets

d) *The pictures in Lesson 4: What is Mr Brown doing?*

1. Mr Brown (to sit) in his sitting-room 2. He (to enjoy) his book? No, he isn't. 3. He (to look) at the evening paper? No, he isn't. 4. What he (to do)? 5. He (to do) nothing 6. Mr Brown (to paint) the bathroom wall? Yes, he is.

e) *The pictures in Lesson 5*

1. Mr Turner (to come) home 2. Mrs Turner (to wait) at the door for him 3. *The picture on the left:* Mr and Mrs Turner (to stand) in their bathroom 4. Mr Turner (to show) Mrs Turner the red spots on his body

3. Say what the people are not doing

The pictures in Lesson 6

Example: The people (to wait) for a taxi?
Are the people waiting for a taxi?
No, they aren't waiting for a taxi.

1. They (to smile)? No, ... 2. They (to have) tea? No, ... 3. The bus (to come)? No, ... 4. You (to wait) for the bus, too? No, I ... 5. The young man (to run) away? No, ... 6. Betsy (to laugh)? No, ...

4. Setze die Verlaufsform ein (Use the continuous form)

1. Betsy (to stand) in front of the mirror 2. She (to put on) her dress 3. Her mother (to sit) in the next room 4. She (to enjoy) the TV programme 5. They (to show) an entertaining film 6. Her mother (to laugh) and (to rub) her hands with pleasure 7. The film is finished. Betsy's mother calls: "Betsy, we (to have) tea 8. You (to come)?" 9. Betsy answers: "No, Mother, I (not to come); I (to wait) for Tom" 10. Betsy's mother enters the bathroom. What Betsy (to do)? 11. Betsy (to put on) her yellow hat. She has a green dress and red shoes on. 12. Betsy's mother says: "My poor girl, what you (to do)? Those colours are awful."

5. Translate

Setze die schräg gedruckten Zeitwörter in die Verlaufsform

Mutter: Geh Herrn Turner besuchen, Betsy. Er ist krank. Er hat [die] Röteln.

Betsy: Arme Frau Turner.

Mutter: Warum arme Frau Turner?

Betsy: Ihre Ferien sind verdorben.

Mutter: Hier ist ein Korb mit Kuchen und Obst für Herrn Turner.

Betsy: Danke, Mutter. Auf Wiedersehen.

(An der Ecke)

Tom: Hallo, Betsy. Wohin *gehst* du?

Betsy: Ich *gehe* zu Herrn Turner. Er ist krank. Er hat [die] Röteln.

Tom (lachend): Ist Herr Turner ein Baby? Babies bekommen *(get)* [die] Röteln. Wie wär's mit dem Kino, Betsy?

Betsy: Was wird gespielt, Tom?

Tom: ‚Das Grüne Monstrum'. Herr Dent, der Schauspieler, ist das Monstrum.

Betsy: Es tut mir leid, Tom, aber ich habe keine Zeit. Herr Turner *wartet.*

Tom: Trinken wir etwas. Es gibt eine Imbißstube um die Ecke.

Betsy: Fein, Tom. Laß uns dorthin gehen.

7 A Letter

1. Fill in the right words

at, back, book, bored, dining-room, in, lavatory, new, parents', phone, plays, spend, visitors, writes

Dear Dudley,

At last we are in our (1) … home. It is in the same road as my (2) … house. Downstairs we have a sitting-room, a (3) … and a kitchen, upstairs three bedrooms and a bathroom with a (4) … There is a little front garden, but we have a (5) … garden, too.

(6) … the evening we are often (7) … home. (8) … are welcome, but even without friends' visits we are never (9) … Shirley (10) … a letter or reads a (11) …, and sometimes she (12) … the piano.

Come and (13) … an evening with us. Write or (14) … before you come. All the best,

Yours, Charlie

2. Setze die richtigen Verhältniswörter ein

1. Mr Turner is standing ... the bus stop. 2. He is waiting ... a bus. 3. It is two days ... his holidays. 4. ... last the bus comes ... the corner. 5. It stops ... every crossing. 6. When Mr Turner comes home ... the office ... the evening, he is always tired. 7. Mrs Turner is ... home. 8. She is ... the sitting-room. 9. Mr Turner knocks ... the door. 10. Mrs Turner looks ... her husband. 11. She says: "You have red spots ... your hands."

3. What Shirley does every day

Setze die schräg gedruckten Wörter an den Satzanfang

Example: She hears the train *every minute.*
Every minute she hears the train.

1. Shirley's day begins *at seven.* 2. She has a hot bath *at eight.* 3. She shuts her eyes with pleasure *when she is in her bath.* 4. She waters the flowers in the garden *at nine.* 5. She phones her friend Betsy *at ten.* 6. She calls on her sister *at eleven.* 7. She has a snack *at twelve.* 8. She takes a bus to the City *at two.* 9. She fetches a newspaper for her husband *sometimes.* 10. Charlie and Shirley have tea *at six.* 11. They often have visitors *in the evening.* 12. Shirley sometimes plays the piano *when she is bored.* 13. The visitors say good-bye *just after ten.* 14. Shirley and Charlie are in bed *before eleven.*

4. Bilde Sätze (Form sentences)

a) *when*

Example: The programme is good; Mr Brown enjoys TV.
When the programme is good, Mr Brown enjoys TV.

1. Mrs Brown is out; Mr Brown begins to paint. 2. The boss is away; the typists like the office better. 3. The buses are full; I take a taxi. 4. The traffic lights are red; the car stops. 5. The traffic lights are green; the car drives on. 6. Her grandma is ill; Betsy goes and sees her.

b) *as*

Example:

Mr Sim is ill; Ann brings him his tea.
As Mr Sim is ill, Ann brings him his tea.

1. Mr Turner is tired; he takes a hot bath. 2. The water is just right; he enjoys his bath. 3. His body is covered with red spots; he jumps out of the bath. 4. The spots are still there; he calls his wife. 5. Mr Turner has German measles; their holidays are spoilt. 6. They have no holidays; they spend their evenings with Charlie.

5. Lies die folgenden Zahlen laut (Read the following numbers aloud)

Example:

13 + 14 = 27   Thirteen and fourteen are twenty-seven.

15 + 16 = 31; 17 + 18 = 35; 19 + 20 = 39; 21 + 22 = 43;
24 + 25 = 49; 26 + 27 = 53; 29 + 30 = 59; 31 + 32 = 63;
34 + 40 = 74; 41 + 45 = 86; 45 + 46 = 91; 49 + 51 = 100.

8 Charlie's New Home

1. Fill in the right words

afternoon, begins, come, coming, gets, goes, going, happening, loves, meet, open, outside, pass, passing, play, playing (2×), shaking

It is a Saturday (1) … Shirley and Charlie are having tea in their living-room. The windows are (2) …

Charlie: Listen! A train is coming.

Shirley: No, it's (3) …

Charlie: Never mind! They (4) … and go every minute.

Shirley: The furniture is (5) … What's (6) …?

Charlie: Two trains are (7) … They always (8) … at this time.

Shirley: Oh yes, they usually (9) … here. (*She* (10) … *up,* (11) … *to the piano and* (12) … *to play.)*

Charlie: What are you (13) …?

Shirley: I'm (14) … 'Oh, how lovely is the night'. *(Suddenly a dog howls* (15) …*)*

Neighbour's voice: I'm sorry, Shirley, but Wolf (16) … it when you (17) … the piano. That's why he howls. What about a drink, you two? Are you (18) … over?

2. Betty is showing pictures to her friend

Example:

Look, Mr Dent (to drive) to the theatre in his new car.
Look, Mr Dent *is driving* to the theatre in his new car.
He (to drive) his new car every day.
He *drives* his new car every day.

1. Look, my mother (to water) the flowers in our garden. She always (to water) them in the afternoon.
2. Look, my father (to hang up) a curtain. He often (to do) things in the house.
3. Look, I (to enter) the stationer's opposite my office, I (to go) to that shop every day.
4. Look, Bill and Sally (to take) a taxi. They seldom (to take) a taxi.
5. Here I (to stand) in front of the mirror. I often (to stand) in front of it.
6. And here Betsy (to play) with her dog. She usually (to play) with it on Sundays.
7. This is Shirley. She (to write) a letter. She never (to write) letters when Charlie is at home.
8. Look, I (to phone) Tom. I always (to phone) when the boss is away.

3. Continuous form or ordinary form?

1. (to write) Shirley … a letter every day. Look, she … now. 2. (to play) Mrs Turner … the piano now. She always … when her husband is not in. 3. (to talk) Listen, these two ladies … about their neighbour. They often … about her. 4. (to read) Now Mr Brown … the newspapers. He always … a newspaper at his office. 5. (to phone) Tom … his mother every Sunday, but now he … Betty. 6. (to drive) Look, Bill … to the West End. He usually … to the West End on Saturdays.

4. Setze die unbestimmten Zeitangaben ein

Example:

People (to wait) at the bus stop (often).
People *often wait* at the bus stop.

1. Mr Brown (to water) the flowers in his garden (never) 2. Tom (to read) The Times (sometimes) 3. Betty (to buy) picture postcards (seldom) 4. Bill (to take) a taxi (sometimes) 5. Mrs Sim (to have) a drink in the evening (always) 6. Betsy (to go) out without her dog (never) 7. Charlie (to spend) an evening with Aunt Sarah (seldom) 8. Mr Smith (to talk) about politics (often)

5. Translate

Am Telefon *(On the Phone)*

Tom: Charlie, bist du es? Was tust du?
Charlie: Ich hänge die Vorhänge auf. Und was tust du?
Tom: Ich lese gerade ein Buch. Es ist langweilig. Hast du Besucher?
Charlie: Mrs Brown und Shirley reden über ihre Ferien. Das ist immer interessant.
Tom: Ich höre einen Hund. Ist es euer Hund?
Charlie: Es ist Mrs Browns Hund. Ich höre ein Geräusch im Telefon.
Tom: Ich esse gerade einen Keks. *(Er hört die Züge.)* Was ist das?
Charlie: Ein Zug fährt gerade vorbei. Die Züge kommen jede Minute.
Tom: Wie schrecklich! Armer Mann!
Charlie: Wir nehmen keine Notiz, da die Miete billig ist. Meine Frau ruft mich. Bitte ruf wieder an. Auf Wiedersehen!

9 The Big Store

1. Fill in the right words

because, breakfast, course, customer, drivers, know, married, midnight, phone, provide, provides, shop, wedding

Do you (1) … Harrods? When you are in London go and see this big store. It can (2) … everything. Do you know who the most important (3) … is? It is the Queen. Does she (4) … at Harrods? Of (5) … she does.

Do you want to get (6) …? The big store (7) … the (8) … dress, the flowers, the cars with (9) …, in fact everything. You can't go to the store (10) … it's too far? Never mind! (11) … the order department even after (12) …, and you can have your bacon in time for (13) …

2. Questions on the text

1. Why must you go and see Harrods when you are in London?
2. What can you do with your dog when you shop at Harrods?
3. What can you do to pass the time?
4. What does the big store provide when you want to get married?
5. What can you do when you have no time to go to the store?

3. Stelle Fragen, die zu den Antworten passen (Ask questions to fit the answers)

1. …….? Yes, the big store sells everything.
2. …….? Dogs must wait in the dogs' waiting-room.
3. …….? The Queen is Harrods' most important customer.
4. …….? Go to the restaurant or take a golf lesson.
5. …….? Yes, the big store provides everything for a wedding.
6. …….? Yes, the big store can even provide the bride.
7. …….? Yes, you can phone the order department even after midnight.
8. …….? Yes, Harrods sell a lot of coffins.

4. Betty goes to Harrods. She wants a lot of things for her wedding.

a) *What she wants*	*What she asks*	*What the assistant says*
Example: She wants a wedding dress.	Do you sell wedding dresses?	Yes, we do.
1. She wants a white hat.	....	....
2. She wants white shoes.	....	....
3. She wants wine.	....	....
4. She wants flowers.	(provide)	....
5. She wants a waiter.	(provide)	....
6. She wants a car with driver.	(provide)	....
7. She wants a hairdresser.	(provide)	....
8. She wants a wedding cake.	(provide)	....

b) *Tom, her future husband, thinks: "These things are so expensive." He says to his mother:*

1. Why doesn't Betty put on her Sunday clothes for the wedding?
2. .... (to take flowers from the garden)?
3. .... (to drive to the church in my car)?
4. .... (to ask her brother to be the hairdresser)?
5. .... (to ask her mother to provide the wedding cake)?

c) *Tom's mother says:*

1. Why don't you tell Betty to put on her Sunday clothes for the wedding?
2. Why .... to take flowers from the garden?
3. Why .... (go on)

5. Beantworte die Fragen sinngemäß in ganzen Sätzen

Customer: Can I have a golf lesson?
Assistant: Yes, (1)... The lesson begins in forty minutes.

Customer: Can I have a tennis lesson, too?

Assistant: Yes, (2)..., but not today.

Customer: Why can't I have a tennis lesson today?

Assistant: You (3)... because the trainer is ill.

Customer: Can I wait in the restaurant upstairs?

Assistant: Yes, (4) …

Customer: Can we have tea together?

Assistant: No, (5) … I'm sorry.

Customer: Can't we have an evening out?

Assistant: No, (6) … My husband waits at the entrance every evening.

10 At the Marriage Agency

1. Fill in the right words

age, difficult, do, doesn't, don't, easy, hesitate, hurry, make, money, name, often, only, overdue, rarely, seldom, tell, watch, woman

A young (1) … enters the office of the Wimbledon Marriage Agency.

Young woman: My (2) … is Betty Brown. I want –

Mrs Baker: Don't (3) … me what you want. I know – Tell me your (4) …

Betty Brown: I'm twenty-five. But I don't know why –

Mrs Baker: Don't be in a (5) … Don't (6) … to answer all my questions. Do you often (7) … television?

Betty Brown: No, I (8) … There's (9) … a good programme on.

Mrs Baker: Do you find it (10) … to talk to strangers at parties?

Betty Brown: I don't find it (11) … to talk to strangers, but I (12) … go to parties.

Mrs Baker: Are you (13) … bad-tempered?

Betty Brown: I'm (14) … bad-tempered when I don't get my early morning tea.

Mrs Baker: Does your mother bring your tea?

Betty Brown: No, she (15) … live in London.

Mrs Baker: Does your father (16) … the morning tea?

Betty Brown: No, my father lives with my mother.

Mrs Baker: Well, your brother or sister, then?

Betty Brown: No, my husband!

Mrs Baker: Your husband? What can I (17) … for you, Mrs Brown? This is a marriage agency.

Betty Brown: The rent for your office is (18) … My husband wants to know whether he can have the (19) … soon.

2. What the Browns can do and what they can't

Example:

Mr Brown can paint the bathroom, but he (to play the piano)
Mr Brown can paint the bathroom, but *he can't play the piano.*

1. His wife can sing, but (to drive a car) 2. She can play tennis, but (to play golf) 3. Mr Brown can speak English, but (to speak German) 4. Mrs Brown can read a German newspaper, but (to pronounce the words) 5. Mr Brown can buy a cheap car, but (to buy an expensive motorboat) 6. Mr Brown can hang up a curtain, but (to nail down a carpet)

3. At the Marriage Agency Mrs Baker wants to know:

1. whether John Green wants to marry a German girl,
2. whether he is a shop assistant,
3. whether he drives a car,
4. whether he goes on holiday every year,
5. whether he lives in a new house,
6. whether he likes politics,
7. whether he thinks that money is important,
8. whether he wants a lot of children,
9. whether he is often bad-tempered.

a) *Mrs Baker says:*	*John answers:*
1. Do you want to marry a German girl?	No, I don't.
2. Are you a shop assistant?	No, I'm not.
(go on)	

b) *Mrs Baker writes down her questions and John's answers. The next customer is Betsy Black. Mrs Baker shows her the questions and answers.*

Betsy asks:	*Mrs Baker answers:*
1. Doesn't he want to marry a German girl?	No, he doesn't.
2. Isn't he a shop assistant?	No, ...
(go on)	

4. Translate

a) 1. Charlie mag [das] Fernsehen nicht. 2. Er sagt: „Ist es nicht langweilig, deine Zeit vor dem Fernsehapparat *(TV set)* zu verbringen? 3. Natürlich kannst du gute Schauspieler, interessante Städte *(cities),* und hübsche Mädchen sehen. 4. Aber ich genieße das Programm nicht, weil ich nicht mit meinen Freunden sprechen kann. 5. Sie sitzen in meinem neuen Wohnzimmer und trinken meinen Whisky. 6. Sie lachen nicht, sie sagen nicht ein Wort. 7. Fernsehen ist nicht gut für meine Augen und es ist nicht gut für Shirleys Figur. 8. Was kann ich tun? Haben Sie eine Idee?“
b) 1. Frau Turner geht gern in *(to)* die großen Kaufhäuser. 2. Warum geht sie nicht in *(to)* ein kleines Geschäft? 3. Sie denkt, daß die verschiedenen Abteilungen im großen Kaufhaus alles beschaffen können. 4. Heute möchte Frau Turner ein Kleid für ihre Schwester, Süßigkeiten für die Kinder ihrer Schwester, ein Hemd für ihren Mann, weiße Farbe für ihr Badezimmer und neue Schuhe kaufen. 5. Es ist schwierig die richtigen Schuhe zu finden. 6. Nach zwei Stunden hat sie ihre schönen Schuhe und ein schreckliches Kopfweh. 7. Sie ist müde, aber glücklich *(happy).*

5. um zu + Grundform (Infinitiv) = to + Grundform

1. Was macht (tut) ihr gerade, Kinder? – Wir gehen nach oben, um unseren Hund zu holen. 2. Ich gehe in mein Zimmer, um ein englisches Buch zu lesen. 3. Mein Bruder begießt die Blumen, um [sich] die Zeit zu vertreiben. 4. Meine Schwester geht gerade an die Theaterkasse, um Karten zu kaufen. 5. Der Lehrer nimmt gerade die Kreide, um an die Tafel zu schreiben.

Test I

1. Pronunciation

Find the same sound (Laut) **as that underlined in the sentence**

1. Can I have that chair?

☐ a) again ☐ b) car ☐ c) carry ☐ d) where

2. These flowers are lovely.

☐ a) know ☐ b) own ☐ c) howl ☐ d) window

3. She had very blue **eye**s.
   - ☐ a) wh**i**te
   - ☐ b) d**ay**
   - ☐ c) Shirl**ey**'s
   - ☐ d) r**ai**lway

4. She has a hot b**a**th every day.
   - ☐ a) l**o**ve
   - ☐ b) m**u**st
   - ☐ c) w**a**rmth
   - ☐ d) l**au**gh

5. We say n**o**thing about the children's noise.
   - ☐ a) n**o**t
   - ☐ b) n**o**tice
   - ☐ c) in fr**o**nt
   - ☐ d) cl**o**thes

2. Stress

Underline the syllable (Silbe) **which has the main stress** (Hauptakzent)

1. suc/cess/ful	6. hair/dress/er	11. mo/tor/boat
2. fur/ni/ture	7. de/part/ment	12. en/ter/tain/ing
3. some/times	8. fac/to/ry	13. ar/ti/cle
4. u/su/al/ly	9. tel/e/vi/sion	14. dif/fi/cult
5. res/tau/rant	10. a/gen/cy	15. hes/i/tate

3. Vocabulary

Mark the correct answer with a cross ☒

1. Shirley is Charlie's …
   - ☐ a) wife
   - ☐ b) woman
   - ☐ c) girl
   - ☐ d) lady

2. Charlie is Shirley's …
   - ☐ a) man
   - ☐ b) husband
   - ☐ c) gentleman
   - ☐ d) bride

3. What about the …? There's 'The Green Monster' on at the Empire.
   - ☐ a) picture
   - ☐ b) cinemas
   - ☐ c) film
   - ☐ d) pictures

4. Let's … a taxi.
   - ☐ a) drive
   - ☐ b) take
   - ☐ c) go with
   - ☐ d) drive with

5. Bill and Sally are … tea.
   - ☐ a) passing
   - ☐ b) eating
   - ☐ c) waiting
   - ☐ d) having

6. Do you want to … your dog at home?
   - ☐ a) let
   - ☐ b) leave
   - ☐ c) bring
   - ☐ d) carry

7. Do you like to ... television?

☐ a) see ☐ b) look ☐ c) look around ☐ d) watch

8. That's a difficult question to ...

☐ a) repeat ☐ b) answer ☐ c) pronounce ☐ d) speak

9. He ... shoes before he goes to bed.

☐ a) puts on his ☐ b) takes off the ☐ c) puts out the ☐ d) takes off his

10. Betty doesn't ... dance because she hasn't much time.

☐ a) always ☐ b) seldom ☐ c) often ☐ d) rarely

4. Structures

Mark the correct answer with a cross ☒

1. Why don't you shop ... Harrods?

☐ a) by ☐ b) with ☐ c) at ☐ d) in

2. My father lives ... London.

☐ a) at ☐ b) on ☐ c) about ☐ d) in

3. Women often talk ... new clothes.

☐ a) about ☐ b) on ☐ c) from ☐ d) for

4. Many people have a bath ... breakfast.

☐ a) in front of ☐ b) before ☐ c) for ☐ d) behind

5. Some ladies are waiting ... the bus stop.

☐ a) for ☐ b) on ☐ c) at ☐ d) after

6. Mrs Turner has red spots ... her body.

☐ a) on ☐ b) at ☐ c) for ☐ d) over

7. ... are awful colours. I can't look at them.

☐ a) This ☐ b) There ☐ c) That ☐ d) Those

8. ... a lot of people in that snack-bar.

☐ a) There is ☐ b) There's ☐ c) There are ☐ d) They are

9. I rarely ... because I haven't much time.

☐ a) don't dance ☐ b) am dancing ☐ c) dance ☐ d) am not dancing

10. He ... it easy to talk to strangers.

- ☐ a) don't find
- ☐ b) not find
- ☐ c) doesn't find
- ☐ d) finds not

11. The trains ... every minute.

- ☐ a) are not passing
- ☐ b) aren't passing
- ☐ c) don't pass
- ☐ d) pass not

12. Shirley ... the piano in the evening.

- ☐ a) plays often
- ☐ b) often plays
- ☐ c) often is playing
- ☐ d) is playing often

13. She always ... to the office.
She never ... the bus.

- ☐ a) is walking – takes
- ☐ b) is walking – is taking
- ☐ c) walks – takes
- ☐ d) walks – is taking

14. Bill usually ... to the office.
Today he ... the bus.

- ☐ a) is driving – takes
- ☐ b) drives – is taking
- ☐ c) drives – takes
- ☐ d) is driving – is taking

15. Listen! A train ...
They always ... at this time.

- ☐ a) is coming – are passing
- ☐ b) comes – pass
- ☐ c) comes – are passing
- ☐ d) is coming – pass

16. The trains ... and ... every minute.

- ☐ a) come – go
- ☐ b) are coming – go
- ☐ c) are coming – going
- ☐ d) come – are going

17. They ... at this time.

- ☐ a) are meeting usually
- ☐ b) usually meet
- ☐ c) are usually meeting
- ☐ d) meet usually

5. Comprehension

Mark the best answer with a cross ☒

1. Our holidays are spoilt.

- ☐ a) I love it.
- ☐ b) Let's have a drink instead.
- ☐ c) I'm sorry.
- ☐ d) I don't know.

2. Where is Tom?

- ☐ a) An assistant.
- ☐ b) Betty's husband.
- ☐ c) An actor.
- ☐ d) In the stationer's shop.

3. What about a drink?
- ☐ a) You're getting on my nerves.
- ☐ b) Stop that noise, Bill.
- ☐ c) Better luck next time.
- ☐ d) That's a nice idea.

4. Who is Mr Dent?
- ☐ a) Mrs Sim's sister.
- ☐ b) In a West End theatre.
- ☐ c) An actor.
- ☐ d) At a party.

5. Do you do a lot of sports?
- ☐ a) I don't know.
- ☐ b) I'm bad-tempered when I don't.
- ☐ c) Yes, I do.
- ☐ d) Of course you know.

11 A Week at the Seaside

1. Fill in the right words

arrive, background, camera, chance, clears, competition, copies, first, guests, happy, hurries, ladies, nothing, page, send, station, sunny, weather, wins

Monday: It is the Smith family's (1) … day at Brighton. They (2) … at their guest-house near the station.

Tuesday: The (3) … is fine. After breakfast the family (4) … to the beach. Freddie takes his (5) … "What about a photograph with the sea in the (6) …?" Freddy says. They all put on a (7) … smile.

Wednesday: Rain, (8) … but rain. They (9) … their friends picture postcards of Brighton's (10) … beach.

Thursday: Three more (11) … arrive at the guest-house. The weather (12) … up.

Friday: Beauty (13) … on the pier. Has Sheila got a (14) …? The judges watch the beauty parade. Number three (15) … Sheila is Miss Brighton.

Saturday: The Smiths are the Mayor's (16) …

Sunday: At the (17) … Freddie buys a paper. Sheila's picture is on the front (18) … They buy twenty (19) …

2. Where are the Smiths?

Put in *at, near, to, with*

They are (1) … Brighton, (2) … a guest-house (3) … the station. They are not (4) … home. On Wednesday they go (5) … the cinema and spend the evening (6) … friends.

3. Grandmother is phoning Freddie in Brighton

Verwende *to have* mit *to do* oder die Verlaufsform in allen Fragen und verneinten Antworten

Example: you/to have a meal/in the afternoon?
Do you have a meal in the afternoon?
you/to have a meal/now?
Are you having a meal now?

Grandmother: Hello, Freddie. you/to have a good time/in Brighton?
Freddie: Yes. I/to have a wonderful time/here.
Grandmother: you/to have your tennis lessons/after lunch?
Freddie: No, Grandma, I/not to have my tennis lessons/after lunch. You always say it's not good for my health.
Grandmother: you/to have tea or coffee/for breakfast?
Freddie: I/not to have tea/for breakfast. I prefer coffee.
Grandmother: Why/you/not to have tea? Coffee is bad for your nerves.
Freddie: I/not to have tea/because I don't like tea, Grandma.
Grandmother: you/to have a drink/before your meals?
Freddie: No, Grandma, I/not to have/a drink before my meals.
Grandmother: What's Sheila doing?
Freddie: She/to have tea/on the pier. It's her first meal of the day.
Grandmother: What? She/not to have a meal/in the morning?
Freddie: No, she's slimming for the beauty competition next Friday.
Grandmother: She/to have a chance?
Freddie: Sheila thinks she has.
Grandmother: I must stop now. Give my love to Sheila and your parents. All the best. Good-bye.

4. Translate

Wie Freddie seine Zeit in Brighton verbringt

1. Jeden Morgen eilt Freddie zum Strand und schwimmt in der See. 2. Dann geht er zum Pier. 3. Wenn er ein hübsches Mädchen sieht, nimmt er seine Kamera und

fragt: „Wie wär's mit einem Foto?“ 4. Gewöhnlich antworten die jungen Damen mit einem Lächeln. 5. Am Nachmittag spielt Freddie Tennis mit einigen Freunden. 6. Wo nimmt Freddie seine Mahlzeiten ein? In der Pension natürlich. 7. Am Abend geht die Familie zum Pier, wo eine Musikkapelle spielt. 8. Freddie tanzt mit seiner Schwester.

12 Christmas in England

1. Fill in the right words

church, let, light, luck, members, normal, ordinary, parcels, presents, receive, seem, speaking, tape, tape-recorder, traditional, tree, wishes

It is Christmas Eve. The (1) … of the Schmitz family are unpacking their (2) … under the Christmas (3) … One of the (4) … is from England. It is a (5) … They put it on the (6) …:

“This is George (7) … A merry Christmas to you all. In Germany you don't (8) … to know much about Christmas in England, so (9) … me tell you something about it. We do have Christmas trees, but we don't (10) … them until Christmas Day. Christmas Eve is just an (11) … evening: the shops are open until the (12) … closing time. On Christmas morning we (13) … our presents, go to (14) …, and then have the (15) … Christmas dinner.

And now I send you our best (16) … for a merry Christmas and a happy New Year.

Good-bye and good (17) …

Charlotte, Marilyn and George.”

2. Verneine

Example: Karla shows her father the parcel. (her mother)
She *doesn't show* it *to her mother.*

1. Karla shows her father the tape. (her friend) 2. The postman gives the Taylors a letter from Germany. (the Turners) 3. Marilyn hands her mother the Christmas pudding. (her father) 4. Mr Smith passes his wife the wine. (his daughter) 5. Mr Taylor sends Herr Schmitz a Christmas card. (the Browns) 6. Tom sells Betty the Daily Mail. (Mr Sim)

3. Verändere und vervollständige die Sätze

Example: Don't give Betsy the dress. (Sheila)
Don't give *the dress to Betsy, give it to Sheila.*

1. Don't send the Smiths the tape. (the Turners) 2. Don't hand Mr Taylor the flowers. (his wife) 3. Don't show your grandmother these pictures. (your grandfather) 4. Don't pass me the cakes. (our guests) 5. Don't tell a stranger your ideas. (your friends) 6. Don't give the child money. (its mother)

4. s-Genitiv oder Genitiv mit of?

1. Christmas is the (season – joy). 2. The (Taylors – dining-room) is full of guests. 3. The (rooms – the house) look bright with balloons and mistletoe. 4. (Aunt Sarah – husband), Uncle Henry, is wearing a paper hat. 5. (The Taylors – daughter), Marilyn, is playing the piano. She's playing 'I'm dreaming of a white Christmas'. 6. It's (her idea – a romantic Christmas). 7. (Mr Taylor – present) to Uncle Henry is a book, 'The Mouse-Trap'. 8. It's (the book – the year). 9. (Marilyn – present) to Aunt Sarah is a red hat. 10. (Uncle Henry – first idea) is: "Fortunately the big store provides everything. 11. I can go to Harrods with (George – 'Mouse-Trap') and get a blue tie instead." 12. Aunt Sarah thinks: "This awful hat is (the present – the season). 13. I can go to the big store with it. They can get me another hat, (the colour – my eyes)." 14. Uncle Henry and Aunt Sarah put on a happy smile. They say to Marilyn: "Your and (your parents – presents) are always so nice. 15. (A thing – beauty) is a joy for ever *(immer)*. Thank you so much."

13 Landing at Dover

1. Fill in the right words

all, climate, foreigner, gangway, has to, long, luggage (2×), one, other, passengers, steams, straight, turn, wish, without

The Belgian boat (1) … into Dover Harbour. The (2) … are on deck with their (3) … All leave the boat by the (4) … The British subjects show their passports

and go (5) … to the customs; the (6) … must queue at the Passport Control.
Now it is Signora Capone's (7) …

Immigration Officer: Your passport, please, madam. Thank you. How (8) … do you (9) … to stay in England, madam?

Signora Capone: Five days. Who wants to stay long in this (10) …? She now (11) … go to the customs hall. She must open her (12) … "What's this?" asks the officer, as he finds (13) … gold watch after the (14) …, ten in (15) …

The boat train to London leaves Dover (16) … the Italian lady.

2. Stelle Fragen, die zur Antwort passen

a) Ask questions with *who*

Example: …? A passenger leaves the boat.
Who leaves the boat?

1. …….? The porter carries the luggage to the customs hall.
2. …….? Signora Capone fills up a new landing card.
3. …….? The immigration officer asks a lot of questions.
4. …….? Signora Capone has an Italian passport.
5. …….? The customs officer finds ten gold watches.
6. …….? The Italian lady has got presents for her friends.

b) Now ask questions with *what*
Example: The porter carries the luggage to the customs hall.
What does the porter carry?

c) Now ask questions with *why*
Example: *Why does the porter carry the luggage to the customs hall?*

3. which or what?

1. … card must a foreign visitor fill up before landing? 2. There are five people on deck. … is your brother? 3. … is the charge for this suitcase? 4. … of these suitcases are yours? 5. … does Signora Capone answer when the officer asks her age? 6. … does the customs officer find in the lady's suitcase? 7. … can I do for you? 8. … passengers must go to the main office?

4. Setze das richtige Fragefürwort ein: 'who – what – which'

Customs officer: (1) ... of these articles are yours?

Signora Capone: (2) ... are you talking about?

Customs officer: I'm talking about ten gold watches and eight silver cigarette-cases. (3) ... do you want them for? (4) ... do you want to sell them to?

Signora Capone: I don't have to answer your questions. I want to speak to my friends in Soho.

Customs officer: (5) ... do you want to speak to? (6) ... is their name?

Signora Capone: Their name is Torelli.

Customs officer: (7) ... is their address?

Signora Capone: They have a restaurant in Soho.

Customs officer: (8) ... is their telephone number?

Signora Capone: 01-1437 6239. (9) ... do you want it for?

Customs officer: I want to tell them that you're leaving for London on the next train. (10) ... do you say to that?

Signora Capone: You're very kind. At (11) ... time does the next train leave?

Customs officer: At 10 o'clock. (12) ... of these cases are yours?

Signora Capone: This is my luggage. Can I have a porter?

Customs officer: Of course.

Signora Capone: (13) ... of these presents can I have back?

Customs officer: I'm sorry, but these articles must stay here.

5. Translate

Der (Schiffs-)Anschlußzug von Dover kommt in London an.

Carlo: Hallo, Mutter! Nett dich zu sehen.

Signora Capone: Hallo, Carlo! *(Sie gibt ihm einen Kuß.)*

(Fünf Kinder stehen hinter Carlo. Sie heißen ihre Großmutter mit Lächeln und Küssen willkommen.)

Carlo: Warum bist du so traurig, Mutter?

Signora Capone: Ich habe keine Geschenke für euch. Es tut mir leid.

Carlo: Was? Keine Geschenke? Wo sind die 10 goldenen Uhren und die acht Zigarettenetuis? Welcher Gepäckträger hat dein Gepäck?

Signora Capone: Die Geschenke für euch sind nicht in meinem Gepäck.

Carlo: Wo sind sie?

Signora Capone: Beim Zoll in Dover. Welchen Bus nehmen wir?

14 The Ideal Husband

1. Fill in the right words

beside, furnished, get, gets, late, life, married, meeting, off, O. K., on, out, pair, ready, rings, takes, up

Dick and Mary are a young (1) … couple. They have a small (2) … flat. This is a day in Dick's (3) …

Seven o'clock. The alarm clock (4) … Time for Dick to (5) … up. He jumps (6) … of bed.

At ten minutes past seven Mary (7) … her cup of tea.

At half past seven breakfast is (8) … Dick puts the tray (9) … her bed.

At a quarter to eight breakfast is finished. Dick (10) … the tray to the kitchen and washes (11) … the dishes.

At eight o'clock Dick turns (12) … the radio in the bedroom. Then he cleans a (13) … of shoes for Mary.

"Are we (14) … in town tonight, Dick?" – "Yes, darling, at 7 o'clock at the Café Royal for dinner, is that (15) …?" – "Fine, don't be (16) …, even if I am." – "Goodbye, darling. I'm (17) …"

2. In the train to London Dick thinks about his summer holidays

1. He wants to spend his holidays at the seaside. 2. He wants to go (!) to Italy. 3. He wants to drive his new car. 4. He wants to buy a new camera. 5. He wants to take a photo of his wife in her red swimsuit. 6. He wants to see some Italian churches. 7. He wants to enjoy the lovely climate.

He thinks:

1. *I'm going to spend* my holidays at the seaside. 2. I'm … (go on)

3. Dick and Mary have a quarrel

1. Dick wants to go to a snack-bar; Mary wants to go to a restaurant. 2. Dick wants to have a cheap meal; Mary wants to have an expensive meal. 3. Then Dick wants to go to the pictures; Mary wants to go to the theatre. 4. Dick wants to go by bus; Mary wants to take a taxi. 5. Dick wants to spend his holidays in Italy; Mary wants to spend her holidays in Germany. 6. Dick wants to go by car; Mary wants to go by train. 7. Dick wants to go in the summer; Mary wants to go in the winter.
Dick says: "I'm not going to a restaurant!"
Mary says: "I'm not going to a snack-bar!"
(go on)

4. Questions with 'to be going to'

Example: (a hat)? No, I want to buy some gloves.
Are you going to buy a hat? No, I want to buy some gloves.

1. (at the Café Royal)? No, I want to have lunch at Harrods. 2. (to the seaside)? No, the Smiths want to go to Rome for their holidays. 3. (an Italian)? No, Sheila wants to marry a German. 4. (the theatre)? No, they want to go to the pictures. 5. (Christmas at home)? No, they want to spend Christmas at Brighton. 6. (write her a letter)? No, I want to phone her.

5. Translate

Die neue Putzhilfe
1. Es ist halb zehn. 2. Mary öffnet die Tür. 3. Ein junger Mann kommt herein. 4. „Ich bin die neue Putzhilfe", sagt er. „Ich werde heute[4] für[2] Sie[3] putzen[1]." 5. „Werden Sie mit dem Schlafzimmer beginnen?" fragt Mary. 6. „Nein", sagt der junge Mann, „ich werde mit dem Badezimmer beginnen. 7. Dann werde ich das Geschirr spülen, dann werde ich das Eßzimmer, das Wohnzimmer und das Schlafzimmer säubern." 8. Um viertel vor zwölf ist die Wohnung in Ordnung. 9. „Wann kommen Sie wieder?" fragt Mary. 10. „Ich werde nächsten Dienstag kommen. Um halb neun", sagt der junge Mann. Mary ist sehr glücklich.

Revision Exercises I

1. Put into the plural

Example: This is a *picture postcard. These are picture postcards.*

1. There is an *egg* for breakfast. There … 2. There is a *copy* of The Times in the office. 3. Where is that *child?* 4. This is the *box* for Mr Brown. 5. There is a *peach* for you on the table. 6. There is a *fly* on the food. 7. On a *bank holiday* many people go to the seaside. 8. This *woman* must have a very good *husband.*

2. Fill in the possessive pronoun (besitzanzeigendes Fürwort)

Example: Where is Mrs Brown? She is in *her* kitchen.

1. Charlie and Shirley are in … new house at last. 2. "We like … neighbours," says Charlie. 3. "Is this … car?" Betsy asks the young man. "Yes this is … car." 4. Betsy's grandmother doesn't live in the City. … home is near Hyde Park. 5. "Here are two theatre tickets for you and … wife." 6. "Yes, I'm staying at a guest-house near the station. … room is very nice.

3. Use the right form

Example: Shirley, pass the sugar, please. Shirley *passes the sugar.*

1. Freddie, please change the subject. Freddie … 2. Let's hurry to the beach. The family … 3. Have another drink, Bill. Bill … 4. Don't blush in front of the camera, Sheila. Sheila always … 5. Does he always catch his train in time? He usually … 6. Does he buy nice presents for Christmas? He always … 7. Does he reply in English? He sometimes … 8. Does he play cards? He … every evening.

4. Wemfall mit oder ohne 'to'?

1. Don't give … Freddie a cigarette, give one … his sister. 2. Do you show these holiday pictures … all your friends? 3. Why do you tell this … me? Why don't you tell it … your mother? 4. You can't sell this car … your parents. You must give it … them.

5. Send ... him this parcel before Christmas. 6. Bring ... my wife a cup of tea, please. 7. Don't forget to send ... your friends a wedding present. 8. Don't carry your luggage. Hand it ... the porter.

5. Questions with 'do' and 'does'

Example: *Do* the Smiths spend their holiday at Brighton every year?
Yes, the Smiths spend their holiday at Brighton every year.

1. ....? Yes, they go to the beach early in the morning.
2. ....? No, Sheila doesn't have eggs for breakfast.
3. ....? Yes, Betsy's grandmother lives near Hyde Park.
4. ....? Yes, Mary often smokes a cigarette after breakfast.
5. ....? No, the Germans don't know much about Christmas in England.
6. ....? No, Signora Capone doesn't like the English climate.
7. ....? Yes, I want a porter.
8. ....? Yes, the big store provides everything.

6. Vervollständige die Sätze mit der verneinten Form der schräg gedruckten Wörter

Example: Signora Capone *likes* English cigarettes, but she *doesn't like* the English climate.

1. Marilyn *forgets* to buy her friend a Christmas present, but she ... to hang up the mistletoe. 2. Betty *dislikes* the television programme, but she ... pop music. 3. Many people *play* tennis; they ... golf. 4. Miss White *reads* a newspaper every day, but she ... The Times. 5. The Turners *want* to go to Italy this year, they ... to go to Germany. 6. I *live* in Brighton, I ... in London. 7. We *have* three meals daily; we ... wine for dinner. 8. You *can* drink a bottle of whisky for breakfast, but then you ... drive your car to the office.

7. Ordinary form or continuous form?

Example: (to play) Charlie ... cards now. He ... every afternoon.
Charlie *is playing* cards now. He *plays* every afternoon.

1. (to pass) The trains ... every minute. Listen, a train ... now.

2. (to enjoy) I always … my tea on Sundays. I … it now.
3. (to play) Look, Shirley … golf with her friend. She always … golf with her.
4. (to drive) I … to Hyde Park. I usually … to Hyde Park in the afternoon.
5. (to wait) Who … at the bus stop? Is it your husband? Yes, he always … for me at the bus stop.

8. Frage nach den schräg gedruckten Wörtern. Setze das Verhältniswort ans Ende der Frage

Example: …? I'm waiting for my sister.
Who are you waiting for?

1. …? I come from *Italy*. 2. …? He is going to *Germany*. 3. …? I'm looking at the *beauty parade*. 4. …? I'm dancing with my *neighbour*. 5. …? They are talking about *new clothes*. 6. …? A hot bath is good for *your health*.

9. Frage nach den schräg gedruckten Wörtern: *who – what – which?*

Example: *A lady* wants to speak to Mr Turner.
Who wants to speak to Mr Turner?

1. *That* porter has taken our luggage. 2. *Each foreign visitor* receives a landing card. 3. The *immigration officer* asks a lot of questions. 4. *The English climate* gets on foreigners' nerves. 5. *That green* swimsuit is the prettiest. 6. *This slow music* makes me sad. 7. *Marriage* makes many people happy. 8. *Many foreign* newspapers showed pictures of Ann's wedding.

10. What an ideal wife never does

1. She never smokes in bed. 2. She never forgets to clean his shoes. 3. She never takes money from his pockets. 4. She never talks to him when he's reading his newspaper. 5. She never makes a face when he doesn't like the soup. 6. She isn't sad when he has an evening out. 7. She isn't sorry to be his wife. 8. She never gets on his nerves.
So, if you want to be an ideal wife,
1. don't smoke in bed, 2. don't forget …, 3. … (go on)

11. A day in Dick's life

Beginne die Sätze mit der Zeitangabe
Example: Dick/to get up/7.00 – At seven o'clock Dick gets up.

1. Mary/to get a cup of tea/7.10 2. Dick/to put the breakfast tray beside Mary's bed/ 7.30 3. Dick/to wash up the dishes/7.45 4. He/to leave the house/8.00 5. He/to catch his train/8.15 6. He/to get to the office/8.55 7. He/to phone Mary/half an hour later 8. He/to have lunch/1.00 9. He/to be back at his office/three quarters of an hour later 10. He/to come home from the office/5.55 11. He/to have a light supper/ 6.30 12. Mary and Dick/to watch television/from 7.00 until 10.00 13. They/to go to bed/10.45

15 Under the Roofs of London

1. Fill in the right words

central, decided, did, dropped, floor, hope, inside, looked, miss, narrow, rest, said, sight, step, such, sure, third, widow

"What you need is a good boarding-house," (1) … the old gentleman opposite me in the train. "Go to 83 Warwick Terrace. Or was it 38? No, I'm (2) … it was 83. Very (3) …, near Paddington Station. You can't (4) … it. Nice little woman – a young (5) …, you know – good food, TV and all the (6) …"
At Victoria Station I (7) … to take the Tube to Paddington. I (8) … for number 83 Warwick Terrace, but (9) … not find it. There was no (10) … number in the street. Was there a number 38? Yes, there it was. A cleaner opened the door. I entered the (11) … hall, full of (12) … My spirits (13) … at the (14) … of the thin old landlady. Yes, she had a room free on the top (15) … This is my (16) … week in that dark room. Every time I (17) … into the street I wonder which of these houses has the nice little woman (18) …

2. A German student writes to friends

Setze in die Vergangenheit (Use the past tense)
Example: I (to arrive) at Victoria Station in the afternoon
I *arrived* at Victoria Station in the afternoon.

1. Ten minutes later I (to be) in the Tube 2. At Paddington Station I (to carry) my luggage up the stairs 3. In the street I (to ask) a taxi-driver to take me to a good boarding-house 4. The driver (to answer) that his sister (to have) a boarding-house in the East End 5. I (to thank) him 6. Half an hour later the driver (to stop) in front of an old house 7. A young woman (to open) the door 8. She (to show) me a very nice room on the first floor 9. The terms for bed, breakfast and dinner (to be) £15 a week 10. I (to have) dinner with three other guests: two Italian ladies and an English actor 11. We (to be) very happy together and (to enjoy) a good meal 12. Later we (to watch) a film on television 13. We (to have) a cup of coffee after the film 14. Then we (to turn on) the radio and (to dance) until midnight 15. Of course, we (to talk) a lot 16. This morning when I (to want) to get up, the landlady (to knock) at the door of my room 17. She (to enter) with a hot cup of tea and (to wish) me 'Good morning'

3. Use the past tense

Example: Susi Steinhoff arrives on the boat train at Victoria.
Three weeks ago Susi Steinhoff *arrived* on the boat train at Victoria. She *asked*... (go on)

1. Susi Steinhoff arrives on the boat train at Victoria. 2. She asks a taxi-driver to take her to Brown's Hotel. 3. She wants to book a room, but there isn't a room free. 4. She asks the taxi-driver to take her to another hotel. 5. At a hotel near Hyde Park she books a very nice room with a bath. 6. There she changes her dress. 7. Then she decides to go out. 8. As she needs some presents for her friends, she enters several shops, has a cup of tea in a Piccadilly tea-room, and then decides to go back to her hotel. 9. But she doesn't know the name of her hotel or the street where the hotel is. 10. Fortunately she still has a few pounds in her pocket. 11. She books a cheap room without a bath in another hotel. 12. Then she phones the London hotels near Hyde Park. 13. She tries and tries, ten hotels in all. 14. At last a voice says: "Yes, a Miss Susi Steinhoff is staying with us, but she isn't in at the moment." 15. It's the HYDE PARK HOTEL. 16. Susi doesn't stay another minute in the narrow room without a bath. 17. She hurries down the stairs and asks for the bill. 18. Twenty minutes later she is in her room at the HYDE PARK HOTEL and has a hot bath.

4. Ask questions

Example: ...? No, the student didn't take a taxi.
Did the student take a taxi? No, the student didn't take a taxi.

1. ...? No, the gentleman in the train didn't give him the right address. 2. ...? Yes, the houses in Warwick Terrace all looked alike. 3. ...? Yes, his spirits dropped at the sight of the thin old lady. 4. ...? No, he didn't like his room. 5. ...? Yes, his room was under the roof. 6. ...? No, he didn't meet the warm-hearted young widow later.

5. Translate

1. Der Polizist versuchte *(to try)* die Türen des großen Kaufhauses [zu öffnen]. 2. Eine Tür war offen. 3. Der Polizist trat ein und schaute sich um. 4. Als er zur Möbelabteilung kam, blieb er stehen *(to stop)*. 5. In einem Bett war eine junge Frau. 6. „Was tun Sie hier?" fragte der Polizist. 7. „Ich versuche die Betten", antwortete sie und lachte. 8. „Ich heirate nächste Woche und wollte wissen, ob dies Bett gut[2] ist[1] *(was)*." 9. Der Polizist glaubte ihr nicht.

16 He Says It the English Way

1. Fill in the right words

burglars, cheer, cook, fine, fire, gone, idea, keep, lonely, make, peas, show, since, starved, stole, walk

An Englishman does not like to (1) ... his feelings. Here is a letter from a (2) ... husband to his wife.

My dear Ann,

It is now two weeks (3) ... you went away. At home everything has (4) ... well. We have not (5) ... Mary is a wonderful (6) ... We have had tinned tomato soup, corned beef, tinned (7) ... and tinned fruit for lunch and supper every day.

Aunt Lily has been here every evening to (8) ... me company. Her (9) ... of this is to sit by the (10) ... and (11) ... a face because she does not like the TV programme. I made some rum punch to (12) ... her up. Later I phoned for a taxi because she could not (13) ... home. Well, everything is (14) ... here.

Love from us all,
Jack

PS: There were (15) ... here last night. They only (16) ... your fur coat.

e story had taken pleace in London and had concerned about a young man and his search for a flat in London.
had come by boattrain and there had told him an old man that he known a got home for him
had said to the young man goto 83 Warwick near PS and there he would find a cheap
ding house with a nice warm heated young widow, good food part games and laughter

2. Form the past tense

Example: Jack (not to like) to show his feelings
Jack *did not like* to show his feelings.

1. Ann (to go) on holiday 2. Jack (to think) of her all the time 3. He (to forget) to switch off the headlights of his car 4. Harrods (to send) the bill for Ann's evening dress 5. Bill (to break) the butcher's window 6. Jack (to give) his son a good hiding 7. Aunt Lily (to keep) him company every evening 8. She (to sit) in an armchair and (to make) a face 9. She (to drink) three glasses of rum punch 10. Aunt Lily (to come) back the next evening 11. The cat (to have) her kittens in the best armchair 12. Burglars (to steal) Ann's fur coat 13. They (to choose) the best thing in the house

3. How Ann spends her holiday

1. Ann goes to the beach every morning. 2. She sits on the sand and often thinks of Jack and the children. 3. She often sends them picture postcards. 4. One day an old dog comes and sits beside her. 5. She gives him a piece of cake. 6. The dog has a fine meal. 7. When Ann gets up, the dog gets up too and goes with her. 8. Ann starts to run, and the dog starts to run, too. 9. She goes into a store and comes out at the other door, and who does she see? She sees the dog. 10. What can she do? 11. She gets into a taxi. 12. Who gets in and sits beside the driver? That awful dog. 13. And who gets out of the train at the end of Ann's holiday? That old dog. 14. When Ann comes home the children think that the old dog is a wonderful present. 15. Only Peter doesn't like the new guest.

How Ann spent her holiday

1. Ann *went* to the beach every morning. 2. She ... (go on in the past tense)

4. Bilde Fragen in der vollendeten Gegenwart (Present Perfect) **und beantworte sie**

Example: Ann/to sew the buttons on (No,/not ... yet)
Has *Ann sewn* the buttons on? No, *she hasn't sewn* them on yet.

1. the cat/to show her kittens to the dog (No,/not ... yet)
2. Bill/to send a nice letter (Yes, ...)

3. Mary and Bill/ to starve this week (No, ...)
4. Ann/to go to the seaside for a week (No, ... two weeks)
5. Aunt Lily/to break the armchair (No, ...)
6. Jack/to forget to pay the butcher's bill (No, ...)
7. Aunt Lily/to drink the bottle of rum (No, not ... yet)
8. Ann/to have corned beef for lunch every day (No, ...)

5. Hans Fendel, a German student, visited England

Example: Hans Fendel visited England last winter.
He had never visited England *before.*

1. He saw Dover from the boat. He had never ... 2. He went by Tube to Paddington. 3. He chose a cheap boarding-house. 4. He sent picture postcards of Piccadilly to Germany. 5. He drank his morning tea in bed. 6. He missed the company of other students.

6. Translate

Wenn Dick nach Hause kommt

Mary: Wo bist du gewesen?
Dick: Ich habe das Paket geholt.
Mary: Ist es angekommen?
Dick: Ja. Es ist im Wagen.
Mary: Du kommst zu spät zum Abendessen. *(You're late for ...)*
Dick: Es tut mir leid. Der Wagen blieb stehen *(to stop)*. Die Batterie war leer. Ich hatte vergessen die Scheinwerfer auszuschalten.
Mary: Hast du das Fleisch beim Metzger bestellt *(at the butcher's)*?
Dick: Ich habe den Metzger angerufen.
Mary: Was hast du bestellt? Büchsenrindfleisch?
Dick: Ja, warum?
Mary: Die Turners kommen am Sonntag.
Dick: Letzten Sonntag sind die Browns gekommen! Müssen wir jeden Sonntag Gäste haben?

17 Betting, a National Amusement

1. Fill in the right words

afraid, begin, learnt, least, lend, once, pleased, result, see, serves, teach, time, twice, within, won

It was half past three on Derby Day. The Smiths had watched the race on television and knew the (1) … Mr Smith was happy. His horse was first and he had (2) … £ 200. Mrs Smith was (3) …, too. Her horse was third. Freddie made a face. His horse was fifth. He asked his father to (4) … him a few pounds.

"I'm (5) … I can't," said Mr Smith. "It's the second (6) … this month that you've asked me for money. If you must bet, then bet with me. At (7) … the money stays in the family. You can have a bet (8) … a month."

"Make it (9) … a month, Dad," said Freddie. "And let's (10) … with our first bet now. I bet you ten pounds that you aren't going to shave off your beard this week."

"I'm going to (11) … you a lesson, young man," said his father. "Just wait and (12) …"

On the sixth day Freddie saw that his father's beard had gone. "Here's your ten pounds, Dad," said Freddie with a happy smile. "I hope you've (13) … your lesson," said Mr Smith. "It (14) … you right."

"I had a bet with Mum that you were going to shave off your beard (15) … a week," answered Freddie. "Now I've won fifteen pounds from her."

2. Aunt Lily's birthday party

It was Aunt Lily's sixtieth birthday. There were 21 guests, and they all had presents for her.

1. Jack had a bottle of rum for her.
2. Ann had a watch.
3. Bill had a box of soap.
4. Mary gave her a cake.
5. Mr Dent gave her tickets for the theatre.
6. Dick's present was a radio.

7. Tom gave her a box of chocolates.
8. Mr Smith had writing-paper and envelopes.
9. Mrs Brown gave her some flowers.
10. Mr Brown gave her a book.
11. Her brother gave her a raincoat.
12. Her sister had a pair of gloves for her.
13. Her son gave her a bottle of wine.
14. Her daughter gave her twenty packets of cigarettes.
15. Freddie's present was a camera.
16. Sheila gave her a photograph of the beauty competition.
17. Betty had some sweets.
18. Shirley gave her a suitcase.
19. Marilyn gave her a tin of coffee.
20. Mr Taylor's present was a woollen scarf.
21. Signora Capone had a silver cigarette-case for her.

a) The first guest had a bottle of rum for Aunt Lily.
The second guest had … (go on)

b) Who was the 2nd, 3rd, 5th, 9th, 12th, 15th, 20th, 21st guest?
Example: The second guest was Ann. The … (go on).

3. Put in: 'at, behind, in, of, on, to, in front of'

1. Epsom is a town … 71,000 people, fourteen and a half miles south … London. 2. … Derby Day there are thousands … cars … their way … Epsom. 3. Millions … people watch the race … TV. 4. The Queen and her family arrive … half past two. 5. The race takes place … the first Wednesday … June. 6. The English spend millions … pounds … the Derby. 7. In England and Wales there are horse-races … 58 race-courses, and races take place … 90 days … the year in Great Britain. 8. … three o'clock the race begins. 9. … the corner, Holiday, the Queen's horse, is first. 10. It's a yard … British Beauty, Lord Derby's horse. 11. An Italian horse, Torelli, is a few yards … the second horse. 12. But Torelli passes first Lord Derby's horse, and then Holiday. An Italian horse has won the Derby. Italy is proud … Torelli.

4. Translate

Nach dem Derby

Er: Wie oft wetten Sie?

Sie: Ein- oder zweimal im Monat.

Er: Ich wette mindestens achtmal im Monat.

Sie: Verlieren Sie oder gewinnen Sie?

Er: Ich gewinne oft, aber gestern hatte ich kein Glück.

Sie: Wieviel haben Sie verloren?

Er: Ungefähr 30 Pfund. Es ist das erste Mal, daß ich so viel verloren habe. Könnten Sie mir fünf Pfund leihen?

Sie: Nein. Es tut mir leid.

Er: Warum nicht?

Sie: Ich habe gestern 20 Pfund auf das Pferd der Königin [gesetzt und] verloren.

Er: Wenigstens war das Pferd der Königin an dritter Stelle (Drittes). Mein Pferd war an zwanzigster Stelle (Zwanzigstes).

18 A Ticket to Washington

1. Fill in the right words

any, anywhere, book, busy, call, crashed, dead, death, finally, grass, immediately, missing, mouth, next, stay, stood, surprised, travelled, trip, way, wrong

"I'm flying to Washington tomorrow," said Mr Scott to his secretary. "Please (1) ... the airline and (2) ... a return flight for me." The date was March 31st, 1973. While Mr Scott was on his (3) ... to the airport, he noticed that his flight tickets were (4) ... He returned to his office. "Have you seen my tickets (5) ...?" he asked his secretary. "No, I haven't," replied Miss Baker. "Have you (6) ... idea where you left them?" As Mr Scott could not find them, he took the train for his (7) ... to Washington.
During his (8) ... in Washington Mr Scott was so (9) ... that he did not read any newspapers or watch television. On April 5th, Mr Scott (10) ... back by plane to New York. Some children were playing on the (11) ... in front of his house. They (12) ... stopped their game and stared at him.

While he (13) … there, an old lady came out of the house (14) … door and looked at him with her (15) … wide open.
"Good afternoon, Mrs Miller," said Scott. "Something must be (16) …, but I haven't got any idea what it can be."
"Well, I can tell you," answered Mrs Miller. "Your plane (17) … after take-off. The police found tickets with your name on them in the pocket of one of the (18) … passengers. A policeman informed your wife of your (19) …"
Mr Scott was very (20) … He (21) … said: "Have you got any idea where my wife is?"
"She's gone to your funeral," said Mrs Miller.

2. When were they born?

Example: Ann was born on (3/1/1938)
Ann was born on the third of January, nineteen thirty-eight.

1. Shirley was born on (4/3/1945) 2. Tom was born on (11/4/1951) 3. My sister was born on (13/5/1951) 4. My mother was born on (2/2/1931) 5. My father was born on (21/6/1923) 6. My brother was born on (22/7/1959) 7. My uncle was born on (18/8/1940) 8. My aunt was born on (10/9/1929) 9. My grandmother was born on (15/10/1911) 10. My grandfather was born on (1/12/1905)

3. Air Flights London – Düsseldorf

	Departure	Arrival
Daily	0915	1025
	1020	1130
	1450	1600
	1715	1825
	1915	2025

Times from 1 minute after midnight to 1200 noon are a.m. times. Times from 1201 to 2400 are p.m. times.

Read the times of arrival and departure in a.m. and p.m. times

Example: Departure from London Airport is at 9.15 a.m., arrival at Düsseldorf at 10.25 a.m. (nine fifteen a.m. and ten twenty-five a.m.).

4. while or during?

While leitet Nebensätze ein, *during* steht vor einem Hauptwort als Verhältniswort (Präposition).
Example: The weather was cold *during* the night.
Miss Baker had two cups of tea *while* she was at the office.

1. She calls the tourist office ... he reads the telegrams. 2. He looks for the tickets ... she writes the letters. 3. He had no time to phone ... his stay in Washington. 4. He never read a newspaper ... he was there. 5. He watched TV several times ... the evening. 6. He had several drinks ... the flight. 7. ... Mr Scott went by train, the other man flew to Washington.

5. something or anything?

On the Plane

1st passenger: Is there (1) ... to read? Have you got (2) ... interesting?
Stewardess: Yes, I've got (3) ... interesting. Today's *Times*.
2nd passenger: Is there (4) ... to eat?
Stewardess: Everybody on the plane gets (5) ... to eat.
1st passenger: Don't we get (6) ... to drink?
Stewardess: Yes, you can have (7) ... to drink.
1st passenger: I want (8) ... nice and cold.
Stewardess: We haven't got (9) ... cold.
1st passenger: I don't want (10) ... hot.
Stewardess (smiling): Well, take (11) ... hot and wait until it's cold.

19 A Sunday in Hyde Park

1. Fill in the right words

become, democracy, dream, end, fight, government, kinds, listen, on, over, pure, since, speeches, tall, terrible, weekdays

All (1) ... the world parks are for people who want to go for a walk. Hyde Park is more: on (2) ... a playground for children, on Sundays the playground of (3) ... Political and non-political speakers of all (4) ... make (5) ... on soap-boxes.

What has that (6) … fellow got to say? Let's go and (7) … to him.
"Yes, my friends, I was a hopeless drinker, until one night I had a (8) … My dear old mother said to me: 'Bill, my son, you won't drink from now (9) … Very soon the world will come to an (10) … There will be another (11) … war, the last war, and the devil's (12) … will rule the world.'
I've never drunk a drop of alcohol (13) … I founded the Doomsday Brotherhood League. Everybody can (14) … a member for 50 pence a year. We'll help you in your (15) … against sin, and we'll show you the path to a new and (16) … life."

2. At Epsom race-course

1. Listen, ladies and gentlemen! Who's going to listen to me? 2. You're going to win a lot of money today. 3. Now I'm going to tell you about my dream. 4. Last night my dear old grandma, she died two years ago, said to me in my dream: 'This horse is going to win the Derby tomorrow,' and she told me its name. 5. Here are some envelopes with the winning horse's name inside. I'm going to sell each envelope for 25 pence. 6. Who's going to try his luck? Who's going to buy an envelope? 7. If my grandma's horse doesn't win, I'm going to pay back your 25 pence.

a) Setze das Futur mit *will.* Verwende die Kurzform nach persönlichen Fürwörtern.
Example: 1. Who will listen to me?
2. You'll win …

b) The man sold 200 envelopes. Ten horses ran in the Derby. Twenty envelopes had the right answer inside. The rest of the people had the name of the wrong horse inside their envelopes. They got their 25 pence back. What was the man's trick?

3. If you had a million dollars, what would you do?

Example: I (to stay in this cheap room). I (not to buy an expensive house).
I'd stay in this cheap room. *I wouldn't buy* an expensive house.

1. I (to go) to the office by Underground. I (not to buy) an expensive car. 2. I (to stay) at a cheap guest-house in Brighton. I (not to spend) my holidays in expensive hotels.

3. My wife (to be) a typist or an assistant in a store. She (not to wear) beautiful fur coats. 4. I (to work) for other people. I (not to be) my own boss. 5. I (to write) my own letters. I (not to have) a secretary.

4. Translate

Eine Rede im Hyde Park

1. Wenn ihr euch meiner Partei *(party)* anschließt, werdet ihr Glück und Frieden finden. 2. Ich bin sicher, daß Geld die Welt nicht regieren wird, wenn wir gewinnen. 3. Jeder Engländer wird sein eigenes Auto haben, aber er wird keine Steuern zahlen. 4. Jeder Engländer wird sein eigenes Haus haben, aber er wird keine Miete zahlen. 5. Jeder Engländer wird freie Ferien bekommen. 6. Wer würde das bezahlen? 7. Niemand würde zahlen. 8. Wir würden kein Geld benötigen. 9. Jedermann würde umsonst[2] *(for nothing)* arbeiten[1]. 10. Wenn alle Menschen umsonst[2] arbeiteten, würden wir glücklich sein. 11. Wir würden kein Geld haben. 12. Wir würden kein Geld benötigen.

20 Teaching English

1. Fill in the right words

animals, aren't, ate, beef, cutlet, don't, eat, meat, mutton, ought, pork, puts, steak, tenses, veal, verbs

Mr Walker enters the classroom. "Good evening, ladies and gentlemen. Last week we learnt some irregular (1) ... Who can tell me the (2) ... of *to eat*?" A big Dutch girl (3) ... up her hand and says: "To eat, (4) ..., eaten." – "You are Miss Vandenberg, (5) ... you? Now, what did you (6) ... for lunch today?" – "Flesh", she says. "No, that's wrong. You (7) ... to know that. Flesh is what you've got on your body. You eat (8) ... You see the difference, (9) ... you?"
Then Mr Walker draws some (10) ... on the blackboard, an ox, a calf, a sheep and a pig. Then he draws a direct line from the ox to a (11) ..., and explains that this is (12) ... The calf gets a line that points to a (13) ..., and Mr Walker tells them that this is (14) ... He also tells them that sheep becomes (15) ..., and that pig becomes (16) ... when prepared for food.

2. must – to have to

A Sentence Switchboard

Miss Vandenberg I The students We	must	learn the English language travel by plane attend evening classes understand English

Put the sentences in the switchboard a) into the past tense (1. Vergangenheit) and b) into the future (Zukunft). c) Form also negative statements *(needn't)* in the present tense (Gegenwart).

3. may I – to be allowed to

A Sentence Switchboard

May	the students he the girls she	smoke during lessons? drive your car? join the party? go by train?

Put the questions in the switchboard a) into the past tense and b) into the future.

Example: Was he allowed to drive your car?
Will he be allowed to drive your car?

4. oughtn't you to – shouldn't you?

Example: Miss Vandenberg won't learn the irregular verbs.
a) *Oughtn't she to learn* the irregular verbs?
b) *Shouldn't she learn* the irregular verbs?

1. Miss Vandenberg won't work at a hospital during the day.
2. The Austrian gentleman won't look for a job in London.
3. The students won't translate the paragraph.
4. The teacher won't explain the meaning of "veal".
5. He won't stay in bed.

5. Setze die verneinte Kurzfrage ein

Example: You like a sunny day, *don't you?*
It is cold today, *isn't it?*
It rained yesterday, *didn't it?*
The weather was bad, *wasn't it?*
She'll come tomorrow, *won't she?*

Austrian student: You like London, (1) ...?

Dutch visitor: Yes, the City is very interesting, (2) ...?

French lady (to Italian lady): Your friends went to the cinema yesterday, (3) ...?

Austrian student: They liked the film, (4) ...? It was 'Britain and Europe', (5) ...?

Dutch visitor: They travel by car through nine different European countries, (6) ...?

French lady: Yes, and something happens to them in each country, (7) ...?

Austrian student: The film shows a lot of Europe, (8) ...?

Dutch visitor: It's an excellent film, (9) ...?

French lady (to Italian lady): And the pictures of Rome were beautiful, (10) ...? You'll go and see it, (11) ...?

6. Setze die bejahte Kurzfrage ein

Example: You can't eat your cake and have it, *can you?*
You haven't played tennis today, *have you?*
He couldn't pronounce that word, *could he?*
They wouldn't do that again, *would they?*

1. Waiter, I can't eat the soup with my fingers, ...? 2. The three-course dinner won't take long, ...? 3. You haven't got a nice cup of English tea, ...? 4. The wine doesn't spoil the taste of the chicken, ...? 5. You couldn't give me a better table, ...? 6. The service isn't included in the bill, ...? 7. You wouldn't take German money, ...? 8. There aren't many good restaurants in this town, ...?

7. Bejahte und verneinte Kurzfragen

Example: You know the quickest way to Hyde Park, *don't you?*
You don't know the quickest way to Hyde Park, *do you?*

1. You can tell us the way to the nearest Underground station, ...? 2. You're strangers here, ...? 3. You could ask somebody else, ...? 4. You won't lose your way, ...? 5. The ladies could take a taxi, ...? 6. We can't take a bus, ...? 7. The number 52 bus goes to Hyde Park Corner, ...? 8. The policeman wasn't very kind, ...? 9. A policeman shouldn't be bad-tempered, ...?

Test II

1. Vocabulary

Mark the correct answer with a cross ☒

1. ... is at 1 o'clock.
   ☐ a) Lunch ☐ b) Breakfast ☐ c) Supper ☐ d) Tea
2. We are having ... for dinner.
   ☐ a) flesh ☐ b) cow ☐ c) veal ☐ d) calf
3. British subjects go to the customs; ... must queue at the Passport Control.
   ☐ a) strangers ☐ b) foreigners ☐ c) widows ☐ d) gentlemen
4. The clock is five minutes ...
   ☐ a) fast ☐ b) quick ☐ c) before ☐ d) in front
5. My watch has ...
   ☐ a) stood ☐ b) stayed ☐ c) spent ☐ d) stopped
6. Dick always ... the beds on Sunday.
   ☐ a) does ☐ b) makes ☐ c) cleans ☐ d) prepares
7. I asked if she had a room to ...
   ☐ a) leave ☐ b) give ☐ c) let ☐ d) sell
8. The Smiths ... their guest-house in Brighton.
   ☐ a) arrive at ☐ b) come on ☐ c) come at ☐ d) arrive on
9. Mrs Brown ... her coat ... the mirror.
   ☐ a) dressed – before
   ☐ b) put on – before
   ☐ c) dressed – in front of
   ☐ d) put on – in front of
10. May I ... you ..., Miss Bird?
   ☐ a) bring – home
   ☐ b) bring – at home
   ☐ c) take – home
   ☐ d) take – at home

2. Structures

Mark the correct answer with a cross ☒

1. You … come tomorrow, won't you?
   - ☐ a) can
   - ☐ b) will
   - ☐ c) needn't
   - ☐ d) must

2. We … translate this text, need we?
   - ☐ a) mustn't
   - ☐ b) needn't
   - ☐ c) don't have to
   - ☐ d) should

3. We are going to drink wine, …
   - ☐ a) are we?
   - ☐ b) won't we?
   - ☐ c) aren't we?
   - ☐ d) will we?

4. You didn't see my glasses, …
   - ☐ a) have you?
   - ☐ b) haven't you?
   - ☐ c) did you?
   - ☐ d) didn't you?

5. There aren't …
   - ☐ a) some letters for me, are they?
   - ☐ b) any letters for me, are they?
   - ☐ c) any letters for me, are there?
   - ☐ d) some letters for me, are there?

6. Has he shown … photos … friends?
   - ☐ a) any – to his
   - ☐ b) any – his
   - ☐ c) some – to his
   - ☐ d) some – his

7. Haven't you got … to say?
   - ☐ a) something more
   - ☐ b) anything else
   - ☐ c) nothing more
   - ☐ d) nothing else

8. We … breakfast on Sundays because we don't get up.
   - ☐ a) don't have
   - ☐ b) haven't got
   - ☐ c) are having no
   - ☐ d) have not

9. "… silly," she … me.
   - ☐ a) Be not – said
   - ☐ b) Don't be – said
   - ☐ c) Be not – told
   - ☐ d) Don't be – told

10. If he comes to London, … him … Harrods.
    - ☐ a) I take – to
    - ☐ b) I take – at
    - ☐ c) I'll take – to
    - ☐ d) I'll take – at

11. What ... do if you won £100 on the Derby?

- ☐ a) will you
- ☐ b) you would
- ☐ c) do you
- ☐ d) would you

12. Who ... three glasses ...?

- ☐ a) drank – rum
- ☐ b) did drink – of rum
- ☐ c) did drink – rum
- ☐ d) drank – of rum

13. ... other people smoke ... meals, I never do.

- ☐ a) During – while
- ☐ b) During – during
- ☐ c) While – during
- ☐ d) While – while

14. Our neighbour asked us to come ... for a drink.

- ☐ a) over
- ☐ b) beside
- ☐ c) on
- ☐ d) about

3. Comprehension

Mark the sentence with the same meaning

1. The dog has missed you all the time.

- ☐ a) The dog couldn't find you.
- ☐ b) The dog lost you.
- ☐ c) The dog looked for you.
- ☐ d) The dog was unhappy because you went away.

2. There was something wrong with him.

- ☐ a) He gave the wrong answer.
- ☐ b) He was ill.
- ☐ c) He didn't feel happy.
- ☐ d) He made a mistake.

Mark the best answer to the question

3. Is this anybody's seat?

- ☐ a) I'm sorry.
- ☐ b) I think.
- ☐ c) Try somewhere else.
- ☐ d) I'm afraid so.

4. Thank you very much.

- ☐ a) Please.
- ☐ b) O.K.
- ☐ c) Don't mention it.
- ☐ d) Nothing to thank.

5. Where were you born?

- ☐ a) I'm born here.
- ☐ b) I was born in 1955.
- ☐ c) It's my birthday today.
- ☐ d) I was born in London.

21 Alone Among Millions

1. Fill in the right words

accepted, aim, between, branches, companion, excursion, forward, hard, head, hostel, invitation, longer, near by, obviously, out, treated, unhappy, willingly

Ingrid Müller was a (1) … to an old lady, Mrs Bunby. Ingrid took her (2) … in her wheel chair to the park (3) …, read to her, looked after the dog and cats, and was very (4) … Like thousands of German girls, Ingrid had come to England to learn the language. Although Mrs Bunby (5) … her well, Ingrid was terribly homesick. She (6) … missed the company of other young people.
One day she heard of the *International Friendship League,* with its (7) … office in London and (8) … all over Britain. The League's (9) … was to promote friendship (10) … young people of all nations. Ingrid wrote to the League, and a few days later she got an (11) … to a dance at the IFL's youth (12) … She (13) … it gladly. Ingrid is no (14) … homesick! She works (15) …, and she does it (16) … – and all the week she looks (17) … to Saturday evening or Sunday, to the next social, (18) … or discussion.

2. Put the adverbs in the right places

1. (slowly) On Sunday morning a red car came round the corner. 2. (quickly) The young stranger went to the door of Mrs Bunby's house. 3. (nicely) He greeted Mrs Bunby. 4. (warmly) Mrs Bunby welcomed him. 5. (proudly) Then the young man showed her his car. 6. "Would you like to drive to the park in my car?" he asked. (gladly) Mrs Bunby accepted the invitation. 7. (happily) When Mrs Bunby sat in the car, she said: "Let's all go to Brighton." 8. (unwillingly) The young man drove to Brighton with Mrs Bunby and Ingrid.

3. very or very much?

Example: The young man drove *very* well. The ladies liked the car *very much.*

Mrs Bunby (on Brighton pier): I always enjoy the sea (1) …
Young man: I'm (2) … pleased to hear that. Would you like to have tea?

Mrs Bunby: That's a (3) ... good idea. Thank you (4) ...

Young man: There's a nice tea-room on the pier. Shall we leave you there? Ingrid and I would (5) ... like to go for a walk.

Mrs Bunby: That wouldn't be (6) ... entertaining for me, would it? I'd (7) ... like to have tea with you two. I hope it won't be (8) ... late when we arrive back in London.

4. Different meanings of 'to look'

Put in: *after, around, at, for, forward to, through, under, up*

Mrs Bunby: You'll look (1) ... the cats and the dog when I'm on holiday, won't you?

Ingrid: Of course, Mrs Bunby. I'll look (2) ... them. I hope you enjoy your seaside holiday.

Mrs Bunby: Yes, I'm looking (3) ... it. What's on television tonight?

Ingrid: I don't know. I'll look (4) ... the TV-page in the newspaper. Do you know where the paper is?

Mrs Bunby: No, I'm afraid I don't. I looked (5) ... it this morning, but I couldn't find it.

Ingrid: Perhaps it's between the old newspapers. Did you look (6) ... those papers over there? *(She looks* (7) *... the papers.)* Verdammt!

Mrs Bunby: What did you say?

Ingrid: I spoke German. I don't know the word in English. I'll have to look it (8) ... in my dictionary.

Mrs Bunby: Where can that newspaper be? Look (9) ... the room. *(Ingrid looks* (10) *... the room. At last she looks* (11) *... Mrs Bunby's wheel chair.)*

Ingrid: I've got it. It was under your wheel chair.

5. Adverbs in front of adjectives

Translate:

1. Ich bin schrecklich glücklich. 2. Er ist hoffnungslos krank. 3. Der Wagen ist schrecklich langsam. 4. Das Buch ist gut geschrieben. 5. Die Taylors sind glücklich verheiratet.

6. Translate

Nach dem Ausflug

1. „Ich bin furchtbar müde", sagte Mrs Bunby als sie langsam das Wohnzimmer betrat. „Es war schrecklich heiß im Wagen." 2. „Ich werde eine Tasse Tee machen", sagte Ingrid glücklich. „Es war ein schöner Tag, nicht wahr?" 3. „Der junge Franzose fährt sehr gut", sagte Mrs Bunby. „Aber er spricht schlecht Englisch. Er sollte Abendkurse besuchen." 4. „Er kann ‚th' nicht korrekt aussprechen", antwortete Ingrid. „Er spricht ‚th' wie ‚s' aus." 5. „Sein Englisch ist wie mein Französisch", sagte Mrs Bunby. „Ich kann sehr gut verstehen, was ich sage, aber andere Leute können [es] nicht." 6. „Die Engländer *(the English)* sollten [eigentlich] Französisch leicht lernen. Es gibt eine Menge französische Wörter in der englischen Sprache, nicht wahr?" sagte Ingrid. 7. „Ja, aber die Aussprache ist sehr verschieden", antwortete Mrs Bunby. „Werdet ihr euch wiedersehen *(to meet again)*?" 8. „Sicherlich", antwortete Ingrid glücklich. „Ich habe eine Einladung zum nächsten IFL Tanz bekommen. Ich habe gern angenommen." *(1. Vergangenheit)* 9. „Der junge Franzose wird sicherlich auch da sein, nicht wahr?" 10. „Ja", antwortete Ingrid. „Ich freue mich auf das Wochenende. Der junge Franzose wird mich nächsten Samstag [mit dem Wagen] abholen."

22 Safety Last

1. Fill in the right words

air, beyond, bought, brakes, cash, climbed, drive, efforts, gear, getting, lifted, limit, mountains, off, petrol, preparing, pressed, push, speeding, tank, tried, valleys

"I (1) ... this car second-hand from a car-dealer in Warren Street. I paid £200 in (2) ... Get in, Marjorie, we're going for a (3) ..." Bill (4) ... the starter, put the car into bottom (5) ..., and (6) ... they went. While the car was (7) ... along a narrow country road, Bill looked at the speedometer. The needle was pointing to 70 miles an hour.

They were driving over the (8) ... and through the (9) ... of the Lake District. But Marjorie was not enjoying Bill's (10) ... as a racing driver.

"Don't worry, Marjorie, the (11) ... are good. Look! We are (12) ... near a village. The speed (13) ... is 30. Is that better?"
Three miles (14) ... the village, when Bill was (15) ... for a new speed record, the car suddenly slowed down and then stopped. Several times he (16) ... the starter. The engine would not start. He (17) ... out, (18) ... the bonnet and, with the (19) ... of an expert, turned a few screws. But still the engine would not start.
Finally they had to (20) ... the car to the nearest garage. There the mechanic looked at the engine, then at the (21) ... and said to Bill: "How many gallons, sir? The (22) ... is empty."

2. Setze die Wörter in die richtige Form der Vergangenheit

Example: When Bill (to speed), two policemen (to stop) him.
When Bill *was speeding*, two policemen *stopped* him.

1. Yesterday afternoon, as I (to walk) along Piccadilly, I suddenly (to meet) my friend Bill. 2. "Hallo," I (to say), "Why are you looking so sad?" 3. He (to look) at me and then (to answer): "Yesterday, while I (to drive) along a narrow country road with Marjorie, two policemen (to stop) me. 4. I (to get out) and (to ask) them what they (to want). 5. One policeman (to want) to know why I (to drive) on the right when they (to stop) me. 6. 'I (not to drive) on the right,' I (to tell) them. 'I (to drive) on the left.' 7. 'Please!' (to say) one of the policemen and (to hand) me a plastic bag. 8. The colour in the bag (to change) from yellow to green. 9. 'That's just what I (to think),' said the policeman as he (to look) at the bag. 'Too much alcohol!' 10. They (to take) my name, then (to take) my car and (to drive) off with it. 11. While Marjorie and I (to walk) back to the nearest village, a car (to stop) behind us and (to pick) us up." 12. While Bill (to tell) me what had happened, I (to begin) to laugh and (not to stop) until he came to the end.

3. Translate

1. Herr Walker ist nach Stratford gefahren. 2. Fuhr er mit dem Zug oder mit dem Auto? 3. Er fuhr mit dem Auto. 4. Kann deine Frau Auto fahren? 5. Ja, aber sie fährt nicht sehr gut, sie fährt zu langsam. 6. Ich fahre nie mit dem Auto nach

London. 7. Ich fahre immer mit dem Bus. 8. Wie oft fahren (verkehren) die Busse? 9. Sie fahren jede Stunde. 10. Wann fährt der Zug nach Wimbledon ab? 11. Fährt ihr Bruder mit dem Flugzeug oder mit dem Schiff?

4. Translate

Eine Panne

1. Eines Sonntagabends saßen Ingrid und der junge Franzose im Wagen und fuhren nach London zurück. 2. Sie waren in Brighton gewesen. 3. Der junge Franzose rauchte eine Zigarette, während Ingrid ein deutsches Lied sang *(was singing)*. 4. Zwei Meilen hinter einem Dorf blieb der Wagen plötzlich stehen. 5. „Das Benzin ist ausgegangen", sagte der junge Franzose. „Es tut mir leid." 6. „Was sollen wir tun?" fragte Ingrid. „Mrs Bunby wartet auf mich." 7. „Sie wird warten müssen. Die Tankstellen sind niemals offen an Sonntagabenden." 8. Plötzlich hielt ein anderer Wagen hinter ihnen. Ein alter Herr stieg aus. 9. „Kann ich Ihnen helfen?" fragte er. „Haben Sie eine Panne?" 10. „Der Tank ist leer", antwortete der junge Franzose. 11. „Kann ich Sie mitnehmen? Ich fahre nach London", sagte der alte Herr. 12. Ingrid nahm gerne an. Sie stieg in den Wagen des Fremden, während der junge Franzose ein [langes] Gesicht machte. 13. „Ich bleibe hier", sagte er. „Vielleicht werde ich etwas Benzin bekommen." 14. Ingrid und der alte Herr fuhren ab. 15. Einige Minuten später drückte der junge Franzose auf den Anlasser und fuhr langsam nach London.

23 Friday the Thirteenth

1. Fill in the right words

apologized, applicants, apply, by, clean, confused, engaged, heavy, manager's, managing, ordered, roared, shorthand, superstitious, trembled, up, wash, whispered

Rhona was more (1) … than most people. Today was the great day when she wanted to (2) … for a job with Webber & Co. And today was Friday the thirteenth!
When she stood in front of the big office building, (3) … rain was falling. A car

went (4) … and – splash! – Rhona's (5) … dress was covered with as many black spots as a jaguar. She entered the staff (6) … office, where three elegant young ladies were already waiting. A man, who was sitting behind his desk, looked at her. "Would you like to have a (7) …? Next door on the right." Rhona disappeared. When she came out, she was so (8) … that she went to the wrong door and entered the office of the (9) … director. "Well, what's the matter?" asked the great man as he looked (10) … Rhona (11) … and tried to withdraw as quickly as possible. "Stay here!" (12) … the managing director. "Are you one of the new (13) …? What's your (14) … speed?" "One hundred and twenty words a minute at least." Rhona's voice (15) … "Not bad," (16) … the boss. "Can you make tea?" "Yes, sir, I can," (17) … Rhona. "You are (18) …," he informed her.

2. Bill's car is 'good, big, nice, new, fast, expensive'

a) Bill's car is good.
Example: It's better than his old car.
1. It's (big) 2. It's (nice) 3. It's (new) 4. It's (fast) 5. It's (expensive)

b) Marjorie has an old car.
Example: It's not as (so) good as Bill's car. Bill's car *is better.*
1. It's not (big) 2. It's …

c) Rhona has a car, too.
Example: It's as good as Marjorie's car. Marjorie's car *isn't better.*
1. It's (big) 2. It's …

3. Three applicants for the job

Example: The first applicant looks fresh.
The second applicant looks *fresher.*
The third applicant looks *the freshest.*

1. The first applicant is late. The second applicant … The third … 2. The first applicant is young. 3. The first applicant speaks little French. 4. The first applicant lives far from the City. 5. The first applicant smokes a lot. 6. The first applicant is slim. 7. The first applicant's hair is tidy. 8. The first applicant's German is bad.

4. The three applicants again

Example: The first applicant is confused.
The second applicant is *more confused than* the first.
The third applicant is *the most confused of* the three.

1. The first applicant is elegant. 2. The first applicant is superstitious. 3. The first applicant is beautiful. 4. The first applicant is willing. 5. The first applicant is worried. 6. The first applicant is astonished.

5. Translate

1. Letzte Woche hatte ich Glück. Ich gewann mehr Geld an einem Tag als ich normalerweise in zwei Monaten gewinne. 2. Ich hatte weniger als zwei Pfund in meiner Tasche. 3. Es war zwei Uhr nachmittags und ich war so hungrig wie ein Wolf. 4. Ich hatte noch nicht zu Mittag gegessen und eilte so schnell wie ich konnte nach Paddington, wo ich ein billiges Restaurant kannte. 5. Auf dem Wege kam ich an einem Wettbüro vorbei. Ich betrat das Büro und setzte mein Geld auf Black Beauty, ein Pferd mit sehr wenig Glück. 6. Natürlich war ich noch hungriger als vorher, aber ich war auch hoffnungsvoller als vorher. 7. Ich spazierte länger als eine Stunde durch die Straßen bis ich vor einem Fernsehgeschäft stehen blieb. 8. Ein Fernsehapparat *(television set)* zeigte gerade die Resultate des 2 Uhr 30 Rennens in Epsom: Black Beauty hatte mit *(by)* weniger als einem Kopf [Vorsprung] gewonnen. 9. Ich rief ein Taxi und zehn Minuten später verließ ich das Wettbüro mit mehr als zweihundert Pfund. 10. Ich war der glücklichste Mann in London.

24 A Murder has been Planned

1. Fill in the right words

blankets, crept, crossed, exactly, fast, front, gloves, hastily, liquid, lying, on, poured, remain, silent, sleep, threw, touched, usual, yard

"I'm going to be operated (1) … early in the morning," said Roy Bilk to the night nurse.
"Well, you must try to (2) … now. Good night."

As soon as she had gone, Bilk (3) … back the sheet and (4) …, rushed to the cupboard to get his clothes and dressed (5) …

Then he climbed out of the window into the (6) …

He rushed through the empty streets and in (7) … seven minutes he reached the road where he lived. He (8) … the road, took his key and quietly opened the (9) … door. His dog was (10) … in its basket. Bilk gave it a sign to be (11) … and to (12) … where it was. Then he went up the stairs to his wife's bedroom. She was (13) … asleep. Bilk (14) … to the small wooden table beside her bed where, as (15) … there was a glass of milk. It hadn't been (16) … yet. With his leather (17) … on, Bilk took a small bottle out of his pocket, (18) … the contents, a clear (19) …, into the glass and disappeared from the room as quietly as he had come.

2. At home

a) Many things must be done daily:

Example: the rooms – to clean
The rooms *must be cleaned.*

1. the beds – to make 2. the dishes – to wash 3. food – to buy 4. the children – to look after 5. the dog – to take out 6. the meals – to prepare 7. the vegetables – to cook 8. buttons – to sew on shirts and clothes 9. the children – to drive to school

b) Yesterday the same things were done:
Example: The rooms *were cleaned.* (go on)

3. At the office

a) *Example:* customers – to receive
Customers *are received.*

1. letters – to dictate 2. telegrams – to send 3. advertisements – to write 4. the phone – to answer 5. applicants – to interview 6. business friends – to meet 7. hotel rooms – to reserve 8. flights – to book 9. orders – to confirm 10. bills – to pay

b) *In the evening some employees meet in a pub and talk about their day's work.*
Example: Customers *have been received.* (go on)

c) *The next day at the office will be like the day before.*
Example: Customers *will be received.* (go on)

4. A party has been planned

1. invitations – to write 2. drinks – to order 3. cakes – to make 4. new glasses and plates – to buy 5. cigarettes – to provide 6. flowers – to put in every room 7. the neighbours – to warn of possible noise

a) 1. Invitations *will have to be written.* 2. Drinks will have to be ... (go on)

b) 1. Invitations *had been written.* 2. Drinks had been ... (go on)

But nobody came, for the wrong date had been given. The guests arrived the next day.

5. Learning English

Put the following sentences into the passive voice. (Use *by* only when necessary.)

Example: Foreign students learn English in special evening classes.
English *is learnt* in special evening classes.

1. Mr Walker stops a Dutch student because her pronunciation isn't correct. (by) 2. She repeats the words several times. 3. She looks up the difficult words in her dictionary. 4. She translates the new paragraph. 5. Mr Walker interrupts her. (by) 6. He draws an animal on the blackboard. 7. An Austrian student asks some questions about the Normans. (by) 8. The Normans conquered England in 1066. (by) 9. The Normans spoke French. (by)

25 The Proof

1. Fill in the right words

arrested, attempted, expression, front, guessed, hardly, laid, news, plain, poison, pulled, scratching, sprang, stuck, unconscious, woke

After his operation Bilk was (1) ... for some time. The noise of a lorry in the yard (2) ... him up. He turned his head and saw a man with a serious (3) ... on his face. Bilk (4) ... immediately that the person was a police-inspector. The inspector said that he had bad (5) ... for him. He told him that somebody had (6) ... to murder Mrs Bilk.

The inspector then said that Bilk had talked while unconscious. "What you said was (7) ... enough," he continued. "You spoke of a glass of milk and a bottle of (8) ..."
The inspector had (9) ... finished talking when a (10) ... noise was heard outside Bilk's window. Inspector Brown went to look and saw a little brown dog with its (11) ... legs up against the wall. In its teeth it was carrying a small empty bottle. The inspector (12) ... the animal into the room. Full of joy it (13) ... onto its master's bed, where it (14) ... the bottle on the blanket and cheerfully looked up for praise.
Bilk tried to say something, but the words (15) ... in his throat. Twenty-four hours later he was (16) ... for attempted murder.

2. Fill in: *braces, clothes, contents, glasses, pyjamas, trousers, scissors*

1. In big stores gentlemen's ... are usually sold on the ground floor next to the entrance. 2. The ... of his suitcase were examined by the customs officer. 3. She always wore a pair of pink ... in bed. 4. His ... fell over his shoes, because he refused to wear ... to keep them up. 5. Though she couldn't see well without them, she seldom wore her ... 6. If you want to cut that picture out of the newspaper, you'll need a pair of ...

3. What people said about Bilk

Example: They said: "He's a bad character [ˈkærɪktə]."
They said *(that) he was* a bad character.

They said: 1. "He spends his money on drink." 2. "He treats his wife badly." 3. "Mrs Bilk is an unhappy woman." 4. "Bilk never has a job." 5. "He always drives expensive cars." 6. "He bets and loses money on horses." 7. "He lives on his wife's money."

4. What the nurse told Bilk

Example: The nurse told Bilk: "You'll be operated on at 8.30 tomorrow morning."
The nurse told Bilk *(that) he would be operated on* the following morning.

1. "You'll have to stay in hospital for another two weeks." She told him (that) he ... 2. "You won't be able to drink alcohol for a long time." 3. "A holiday will do you good." 4. "You'll have to be careful not to catch cold." 5. "You'll have to see the doctor regularly." 6. "You'll suffer from headaches for some time."

5. What Bilk told the inspector

Example: Bilk told the inspector: "I haven't left the hospital since my arrival."
Bilk told the inspector *(that) he hadn't left* the hospital since *his* arrival.

1. "My wife has always suffered from bad nerves." He told him (that) his wife ... 2. "I've often warned my wife to be careful with dangerous medicine." 3. "I've never hurt a fly." 4. "My wife has been very happy with me." 5. "I've always been a good husband." 6. "I've never planned to murder my wife."

6. What the inspector wanted to know

Example: The inspector wanted to know: "Do you love your wife?"
The inspector wanted to know *whether (if) Bilk loved his* wife.

1. "Do you spend a lot of money on horses?" He wanted to know whether ... 2. "Does your wife wish to leave you?" 3. "Does she still give you money?" 4. "Are the contents of the bottle known to you?" 5. "Does your dog always bring things to you?" 6. "Are you always so worried?"

7. What the inspector told his assistant

a) *Example:* The inspector told his assistant: "Send a police car immediately."
The inspector told his assistant *to send* a police car immediately.

1. "Take Bilk to the prison hospital." He told him to ... 2. "Examine the contents of the cat's stomach." 3. "Find out whether (if) Bilk was seen in the street last night." 4. "Get some more details about the Bilks' marriage." 5. "Make inquiries about Mrs Bilk's health."

b) *Example:* He told the nurse: "Don't speak to the patient."
He told the nurse *not to speak* to the patient.

1. "Don't give him his clothes." He told her ... 2. "Don't let him use the phone."

3. "Don't give him a knife with his meals." 4. "Don't go into his room alone."
5. "Don't let him know that he's going to be arrested."

26 The Man who was Waiting for his Wife

1. Fill in the right words

addressed, all, ashamed, else, familiar, for, honest, imagine, introduce, manager, no, penny, really, so, story, tricked, true, waitress, wallet

One day I entered a restaurant near Piccadilly to have lunch. At a small table a man was sitting with a sad, but (1) … face. After some minutes he (2) … me, "May I (3) … myself? My name is White, Captain John White. I'm waiting for my wife. I can't (4) … what has happened to her."

"Well, women are often late."

"That's (5) …," said the man, "but I've been waiting (6) … over three hours. I had had a good meal, and after about an hour I decided to go. Then I discovered that I had forgotten my (7) … and hadn't a (8) … in my pocket, so I had to wait for my wife after (9) … Later I had a piece of cake, and now a cup of coffee. If I tell the (10) … now that I can't pay, she'll call the (11) … and nobody will believe my (12) …"

"Don't worry!" I said. "I'll pay the bill for you."

"It's (13) … very kind of you," said the man. "Thank you (14) … much."

Some weeks later I had lunch at another restaurant. As I went in I heard a (15) … voice. It was my Piccadilly friend who was telling his story to someone (16) … At once I knew that I had been (17) … and went straight to his table. But the man remembered me, too. In (18) … time he had disappeared. Was he (19) … of himself?

2. Fill in pronouns with '-self, -selves'

Example: Rhona looked in the mirror and smiled at …
Rhona looked in the mirror and smiled at *herself*.

"That's a nice looking girl," the driver thought to (1) … when Rhona got into his taxi. "I'll try and get a good seat," said Rhona to (2) … as she was driving to the West

End, but when she arrived at the box-office of the theatre, she found (3) … in front of a House Full notice. "Why didn't I get (4) … a ticket yesterday," she thought to (5) …, when suddenly a young man addressed her.

Young man: Excuse me, but haven't you got a ticket? I bought two tickets, one for my friend and one for (6) …, but unfortunately my friend fell and hurt (7) … this afternoon. So he has excused (8) … for the evening. I shan't enjoy (9) … alone. Would you like to have his ticket?

Rhona: Will you enjoy (10) … more if I'm with you? Of course, I can't accept the ticket for nothing.

Young man: I would be very pleased to have your company. May I introduce (11) …? My name is Peter Hartung.

Rhona: I'm astonished at (12) …, Mr Hartung, but I'll accept your invitation. You're not English, are you? But you can be very proud of (13) … You speak very good English.

Young man: I'm German. I make (14) … practise my English every day.

Rhona: I wish I could bring (15) … to practise my French like that. I'm afraid we English often make fools of (16) … when we try to speak foreign languages.

Young man: As long as people can make (17) … understood in a foreign language they can be pleased with (18) … And a pretty girl like you can never make a fool of (19) …

Rhona: Thank you, Mr Hartung. I'm sure we'll enjoy (20) … this evening.

3. Adjective or adverb?

Beachte: *to look* = „aussehen“ und *to feel* = „sich fühlen“ bezeichnen nicht eine Tätigkeit, sondern ein Sein. Sie werden daher – wie *to be* – nicht mit dem Adverb, sondern mit dem Adjektiv verbunden, z. B.
He looked glad. (= He was glad.)
He felt hungry. (= He was hungry.)

Example: The man/to look/happy
The man *looked happy.*
The man/to sing/happy/in his bath
The man *sang happily* in his bath.

1. This exercise/to look/easy. 2. You/to be able/to translate it/easy. 3. She/to feel/

hungry/after her long walk. 4. The children/to eat their cake/hungry. 5. He/to be/hopeless/as a driver. 6. Ingrid/to feel/hopeless/lonely in London. 7. She/to look/terrible/sad. 8. After her first evening at the IFL/Ingrid/to feel/happy. 9. She/to laugh/happy/at the Frenchman's remarks. 10. She/to look/beautiful/in her new dress. 11. She/always to dress/beautiful.

4. Fill in 'remind' or 'remember'

Beachte: *to remind someone of something* = einen anderen an etwas erinnern
to remember something = sich selbst an etwas erinnern

1. I'd like to ... you of what happened to Mrs Bilk's cat. 2. Will you ... me to buy some stamps? 3. Do you ... when we first met? 4. I always forget to ... my wife's birthday. 5. Don't ... father of the day when the dog spoilt his garden. 6. Rhona will always ... Friday the 13th. 7. Will the manager ... to reserve the first floor for our wedding party? 8. Please ... to buy some wine for the weekend. 9. You needn't ... me. I'll ... 10. I don't have to ... my secretary to book my flight to New York. She'll ...

5. Fill in: *about, at, by, for, in, of, on, to*

He: What (1) ... a drive (2) ... the seaside this afternoon?
She: I'd prefer to go (3) ... train. The roads are always full (4) ... traffic (5) ... that time of day.
He: But I'd like to go (6) ... car. We might be (7) ... Brighton (8) ... time (9) ... tea.
She: Think (10) ... the dog. It's always sick (11) ... the car.
He: You needn't worry (12) ... the dog. I'll drive very carefully.
She: Look (13) ... the weather. We're sure to have rain (14) ... the way.
He: Never mind the weather, never mind the rain. Turn (15) ... the radio. They'll tell you (16) ... the weather.
Voice (17) ... *the radio:* There will be heavy rain (18) ... the afternoon. The weather will clear up (19) ... the evening.
She: Shall I put (20) ... my swimsuit?
He: Don't be silly. We're staying (21) ... home. I was really looking forward (22) ... an afternoon (23) ... the seaside. We'll have to wait (24) ... better weather.

27 Journey's End

1. Fill in the right words

ancestor, appointed, barrier, before, career, clever, educated, filled, great-grandson, lack, landed, offered, polite, position, post, study

One day in 1957, John Baker, the (1) ... of a Negro slave, (2) ... at Liverpool. A (3) ... boy, he had attended the grammar school at Kingston (Jamaica) and had decided to (4) ... physics at London University.
When John Baker had passed his examinations he began to look for a (5) ... as a physicist. He applied for dozens of (6) ... with private firms, but the answer was always the same: "We're sorry, but the position has been (7) ..." Everybody was most (8) ... Nobody explained to him the reason for his (9) ... of success. But John Baker knew: a (10) ... stood between him and his (11) ... It was his colour. Then he saw an advertisement in the newspaper. The Federal Government of Nigeria (12) ... positions as instructors to science graduates. Baker applied for a position and he got it. He was also (13) ... professor of physics at Lagos University.
When he landed in Africa, John Baker, a free and (14) ... man, ended the journey which his (15) ... had started as a slave four centuries (16) ...

2. Connect the sentences with a relative pronoun

Example: a) John Baker landed at Liverpool in 1957. *He* had attended a grammar school in Jamaica.
John Baker, *who* had attended a grammar school in Jamaica, landed at Liverpool in 1957.
b) John Baker was born in the West Indies. *His* great-grandfather had been a slave.
John Baker, *whose* great-grandfather had been a slave, was born in the West Indies.

1. John Baker worked as a liftboy at night. *He* studied hard during the day. 2. The young physicist studied at London University. *His* parents worked for sugar-planters in Jamaica. 3. The Negroes in Britain work as bus conductors, nurses, porters and waiters. *They* earn the same wages as their white colleagues. 4. After his examinations John Baker was in despair. *He* couldn't find a job as a physicist. 5. The staff managers

never gave him a job. *Their* answers were always the same. 6. Baker applied for a Government post. *He* knew the reason for his lack of success with private firms. 7. Finally Baker accepted a post as a welfare officer. *His* wish was to become a physicist. 8. One day John Baker saw an advertisement. *He* read the newspapers regularly. 9. Nigeria offered positions as instructors to science graduates. *Her* independence had just been proclaimed. 10. In 1962 Baker became an instructor in Nigeria. *His* journey had started in Jamaica.

3. Fill in the blanks with relative pronouns

1. The staff manager was interviewing three young ladies ... were applying for the position of private secretary to the managing director. 2. The girls, ... were between 18 and 21, all looked very pretty. 3. The managing director entered the room in ... the interview was taking place. 4. He told the staff manager that Rhona, ... he had interviewed himself, was going to be his private secretary. 5. The staff manager, ... job it was to engage employees, was not pleased. 6. "The lady ... you've engaged was sent away to have a wash, because her dress was covered with black spots," said the staff manager. "The applicant about ... you seem so pleased should have come back to my office, ... is the right place for an interview." 7. "I can choose ... I like as my private secretary," replied the managing director. 8. "You only make my work, ... is not easy, more difficult than necessary," said the staff manager, ... had already made his choice – a nice girl with fair hair and a fine figure.

4. Translate

Am Londoner Flughafen

Einwanderungsbeamter:	Können Sie mir erklären, warum Sie England zum dritten Mal in einer Woche besuchen?
Ausländischer Geschäftsmann:	Die Ware *(goods, pl.)*, die meine Firma unseren britischen Kunden liefern mußte, ist nicht angekommen. Ich versuche die Ware, die verschwunden ist, zu finden.
Beamter:	Welche Art Ware?
Geschäftsmann:	Kunststofftüten. Wir schickten sie unseren Kunden vor vier Wochen.

Beamter:	Ich möchte *(I'd like to)* etwas vorschlagen. Informieren Sie die Polizei.
Geschäftsmann:	Ich glaube nicht, daß die Ware gestohlen wurde.
Beamter:	Nein, aber die Polizei könnte Ihnen bei *(with)* Ihren Nachforschungen helfen. Haben Sie eine Idee, wessen Fehler es sein könnte?
Geschäftsmann:	Nein. Die Ware ist irgendwo zwischen London und Glasgow. Unsere Kunden, die in Glasgow ein großes Kaufhaus haben, werden uns nicht bezahlen, bevor sie die Ware erhalten haben.
Beamter:	Nun, ich wünsche Ihnen Glück.

28 The World Food Crisis

1. Fill in the right words

affected, cause, demand, freeze, increase (2×), increasing, pace, particularly, present, rise (2×), solve, sorry

"The only way to stop the (1) … in prices is to have a price (2) …," Mrs Brown told her husband.

Mr Brown looked up from his paper and said calmly, "That won't (3) … the problem, dear. Food prices will continue to (4) … whether we like it or not. The (5) …, which lies outside Britain, is the (6) … world population."

"Why don't they (7) … food production, too?" asked Mrs Brown. "There has been an (8) … in food production, (9) … in India," replied her husband, "but the Indian farmers couldn't keep (10) … with the population explosion."

"Since we in Britain aren't directly (11) … by the food shortage the Third World suffers from, why do prices go up here?" asked Mrs Brown.

"It's a question of supply and (12) …," replied her husband. "The (13) … world shortage of food sends up the prices we have to pay for our bread and meat. Every year the world has seventy-four million new mouths to feed. Therefore, as long as we can buy the food we need, we shouldn't worry about ourselves, even if prices go up. We should feel more (14) … for those who were born to be hungry."

2. The Third World

Example: The lack of food *from which* the Third World is suffering is a most serious problem.
The lack of food *that* the Third World is suffering *from* is a most serious problem.
The lack of food the Third World is suffering *from* is a most serious problem.

1. The population problem with which they have to deal cannot be solved immediately. 2. The people to whom we talked were food experts. 3. The developing countries to which the experts travelled were in South Africa. 4. Birth control is one of the possible answers about which the United Nations Organization is talking with various governments. 5. The diseases of which millions of people died fifty years ago can now be successfully treated by modern medicine. 6. An increase in food production could be the help for which the developing countries are waiting. 7. Modern medicine on which people depend must go hand in hand with increased food production and birth control.

3. Put in the relative pronoun where necessary

1. "Not everything ... you sell is gold, is it?" said Rhona as she looked at the various watches the man was offering. 2. "Everything ... is sold here is gold," answered the man. "Look! The watch right under your nose is something ... you'll like. All ... I'm asking for it is ten pounds." 3. "I want a present for my mother, but all ... I can afford is five pounds," said Rhona. 4. "This is something ... will make my wife angry when she hears about it. I'll give you the watch for seven pounds fifty, because I have a dear old mother myself. What do you say to that?" 5. "Five pounds is all ... I have," said Rhona. 6. "There's not much ... you can buy here for five pounds, young lady." 7. "Think of your dear old mother," said Rhona. "Wouldn't you try to buy something ... would give her pleasure?" 8. "You're breaking my heart! I can't say 'no' to a woman. They always get everything ... they want."

4. Translate

Leave out the relative pronoun where possible
alles, nichts, usw., was = *everything, nothing, etc, that.*

a) 1. Der Redner sagte etwas, was nicht richtig sein konnte: „Alles was [die] moderne Medizin tut, um Krankheiten zu bekämpfen, erhöht die Bevölkerungsexplosion, die eine große Gefahr ist." 2. Das war etwas, was ich nicht glauben konnte. 3. Wir müssen nicht alles glauben, was die Zeitungen sagen. 4. Es gibt nichts, was ich mehr liebe als einen guten Artikel in der Zeitung. 5. Gibt es irgend etwas, was ich für Sie tun kann?
b) 1. Das Restaurant, das ich gestern aufsuchte *(to go to)*, hatte keinen Fisch. 2. Ich entschloß mich zu gehen *(to leave)*. Plötzlich hörte ich eine Stimme, die ich kannte. 3. Ich blickte auf und sah meinen Bruder, der neben einem hübschen Mädchen saß. Ich ging zu seinem Tisch, um ihn zu begrüßen *(to greet)*. 4. Als mein Bruder mich sah, wurde sein Gesicht, das so glücklich gewesen war, plötzlich bekümmert. Er sah verlegen aus, aber er stellte mich seinem Mädchen vor. 5. Dann entdeckte ich den Grund für sein merkwürdiges Benehmen: Er trug meinen besten Anzug, auf den ich so stolz war.

Revision Exercises II

1. Questions with 'did'

Example: ...? Yes, I found a good boarding-house in Paddington.
Did you find a good boarding-house in Paddington?

1. ...? No, I didn't like my room. 2. ...? Yes, I stayed there for more than three weeks. 3. ...? No, we didn't play any games in the evening. 4. ...? Yes, I had dinner at the boarding-house. 5. ...? Yes, the other guests got up early. 6. ...? Yes, we had a cup of coffee in the evening. 7. ...? No, the landlady didn't give me a clean towel every day. 8. ...? Yes, the old gentleman in the train made a mistake.

2. Use the present perfect

Example: (to go) The buttons on Jack's shirts ...
The buttons on Jack's shirts *have gone.*

1. (to be) Aunt Lily ... here every evening. 2. (to write) Jack ... several letters to his wife. 3. (to cook) Mary ... wonderful meals. 4. (to have) The cat ... her kittens in the best armchair. 5. (to spend) Jack is tired, because he ... the evening with Aunt Lily. 6. (to break) The butcher is angry, because Bill ... his shop window.

7. (to steal) Jack's wife is sad; burglars ... her fur coat. 8. (to drink) Aunt Lily is happy; she ... three glasses of rum.

3. Fill in 'some – any'

1. Mr Scott wanted to dictate ... letters to his secretary. 2. Were there ... telegrams for Mr Scott? No, there weren't ... 3. There weren't ... seats left on the next plane. 4. Did Mr Scott read ... newspapers or watch ... television programmes during his stay in Washington? 5. When he heard the news of what had happened to his plane, Mr Scott needed ... whisky. 6. The neighbour hadn't ... idea where Mr Scott's wife was. 7. .. people have all the luck, others haven't ...

4. something – anything, somebody – anybody, somewhere – anywhere

1. Have you got ... for me? Yes, I've got ... for you. 2. Is there ... I can do for you? 3. ... that you told me yesterday helped me a lot. 4. I can't find my wallet. I must have left it ... 5. Can't I find a good armchair ...? 6. ... told me that ... was wrong with my car. 7. Is there ... here who has been to New York this year? 8. There wasn't ... who could tell me where Paddington Station was.

5. Put the sentences into the future *(to be able to – to be allowed to – to have to)*

Example: Miss Vandenberg *can* speak English.
Miss Vandenberg *will be able to* speak English.

1. We *may* smoke during lessons. 2. Ingrid *must* take Mrs Bunby out in her wheelchair. 3. The students *can* translate a difficult English text. 4. People *mustn't* drive at more than 30 miles per hour through this village. 5. You *must* pronounce every word correctly. 6. The ladies *may* choose their partners. 7. *Must* we leave a tip? 8. *Can* you explain why?

6. Fill in the question tags (Kurzfragen)

Example: Ingrid isn't happy at Mrs Bunby's, *is she?*
Ingrid takes the lady to the Park every day, *doesn't she?*

1. Ingrid looked after the cats and dog, ...? 2. She had come to England to learn English, ...? 3. She missed the company of young people, ...? 4. She hadn't heard of the International Friendship League before, ...? 5. She won't be homesick any longer, ...? 6. She didn't tell Mrs Bunby about the young Frenchman, ...? 7. She can dance well, ...? 8. The young people will meet again, ...?

7. Rewrite the sentences below, using adverbs instead of adjectives

Example: It was *obvious* that Ingrid missed the company of young people.
Ingrid *obviously* missed the company of young people.

1. It's possible that the young Frenchman will meet Ingrid again. 2. I'm certain that Ingrid enjoyed her evening at the hostel. 3. It's probable that Bill wanted to show Marjorie how well he could drive. 4. It was surprising that the car did not run into a tree. 5. It was fortunate that the brakes were good. 6. It was obvious that the mechanic knew more about cars than Bill did.

8. Compare

a) *Example:* Rhona was *superstitious.* (most people)
Rhona was *more superstitious than* most people.

1. When she broke the mirror Rhona felt *bad.* (a fish out of water) 2. When a car went by, Rhona was covered with *many* black spots. (a jaguar) 3. The other applicants looked *fresh.* (the morning dew) 4. Rhona's face became *red.* (tomato) 5. When Rhona entered the manager's room, she was *confused.* (a six-year-old child) 6. Rhona's shorthand speed was *good.* (that of the other secretaries) 7. Rhona was *fortunate.* (the other applicants)

b) *Example:* Rhona was *as superstitious as* most people. (go on)

9. Put into the passive voice (use *by* only when necessary)

Example: The doctors will operate on *Bilk* early in the morning.
Bilk will be operated on early in the morning.

1. The nurse turned off *the lights.* (by) 2. She left the *patient* alone. 3. They kept *his clothes* in the cupboard. 4. Bilk had planned *a murder.* (by) 5. He was going

to kill *his wife*. 6. She always kept *her bedroom door* open. 7. One could see *everything in the bedroom*. 8. Nobody trusted *Bilk*. (by)

10. Fill in the pronouns with '-self, -selves' where necessary

1. "May I introduce ...? My name is Captain John White. 2. I don't want to make a fool of ..., but I can imagine ... that you'll say I'm silly." 3. As I had plenty of time, I decided ... to listen to the gentleman who addressed me. 4. "I ought to be ashamed of ...," continued the man, "but I can't remember ... the name and the street of my hotel. 5. I wonder ... whether you could help me." 6. I realized ... that the man wanted money. 7. "I'm a stranger here in London," said the man and sat down ... beside me in the snack-bar where I was having a snack. 8. "I arrived at Paddington this morning and found ... a nice hotel in the West End. 9. I undressed ..., washed ... and then put on some other clothes." 10. "Allow me to tell the rest of your story ...," I said. 11. "You walked through the streets, you enjoyed ... until you wanted to buy ... a drink. 12. You felt in your pockets and found ... without any money. 13. You tried to remember ... the name of your hotel, but you couldn't." 14. "That's right," said the gentleman. "How do you know?" "Well," I told him. "I use that trick ... when I need some money. 15. We think ... very clever when we try to trick other people, but often we make fools of ..."

11. John Baker in Lagos

Example: He gave excellent instructions to his students.
The instructions *he gave to his students* were excellent.

1. He drove an expensive car. 2. He lived in a beautiful house. 3. He wore elegant suits. 4. He chose nice Christmas presents for his English friends. 5. He wrote interesting articles for the world of science. 6. He had to deal with a lot of interesting people. 7. He got married to a very young woman.

12. Fill in the blanks

1. Ingrid speaks good English. She speaks English ... 2. Rhona drives a fast car. She often drives too ... 3. This letter is bad. It is ... written. 4. Your pronunciation is wrong. You pronounce the words ... 5. Your answer was correct. You answered ...

6. You did a lot of hard work. You needn't work so ... 7. That was an easy walk. We did it quite ... 8. This is the daily newspaper. We read it ...

29 The Problem of Automation

1. Fill in the right words

about, boil, causing, computer, development, face, for, labour, on, quite, roll, since, sooner, strike, threatened, trouble, unions

One evening Fred Jones came home looking as if he had lost a pound and found a penny.
"What's the (1) ...?" asked Mary.
"It's those containers that are (2) ... the trouble," replied Fred. "Ever (3) ... they appeared, our jobs have been (4) ... It makes my blood (5) ..."
"Can't you do anything (6) ... it?" asked Mary.
"We're going to (7) ...," replied her husband. "We must stop those lorries. The (8) ... the better. They (9) ... in and out of the docks with the containers while we look (10) ... They call it progress! All they really want is to save (11) ... costs!"
The problem the dockworkers have to (12) ... is automation. In the USA, where automation is most advanced, unemployment has been (13) ... a problem (14) ... years. One (15) ... can do the work of a thousand clerks. The consequences of this (16) ... must be studied carefully.
Employers, (17) ... and the State will have to consider the problem.

2. Answer the following questions

1. How many pence make a pound? 2. How many pence are there in five pounds? 3. What English coins are there? 4. What English bank-notes are there? 5. What is the smallest coin? 6. What may be dropped if a smaller amount follows the pound?

3. Weights and measures

Read: 15 lb. 10 ozs; 10,000 ft.; 6.568 l.; £15.09; 50p; 10 cwts; 1,760 yds 7 ins; 5 gals; 4 qts; 3 pts; 4 st. 6 lbs; 1 m.

4. Professions, nationalities, religion [ri'lidʒen]

a) 1. Mr Smith sells newspapers, writing-paper, pens, pencils and postcards. He is ... (L2). 2. Tom helps him in the shop. He is ... (L2). 3. Miss White works in a City office. She is ... (L2). 4. Signora Capone lives in Italy. She is ... (L13). 5. Mr Scott is flying from New York to Chicago to meet business friends. He is ... (L18). 6. Miss Vandenberg attends evening classes. She is ... (L20). 7. Fred Jones works at the Port of London. He is ... 8. His wife cleans offices in an office building. She is ... 9. Mr Dent is playing Hamlet at a West End theatre. He is ... (L1). 10. This lady goes to the Catholic church every Sunday. She is ...

b) *Translate*

1. Ich wohne in Deutschland, aber ich bin britischer Staatsangehöriger (L13). 2. Der Mann, der morgen nach Rom fährt, ist Katholik. 3. Mr Brown verlor seine Stellung als Zollbeamter, weil die Polizei entdeckte, daß er eine goldene Uhr von einem Franzosen angenommen hatte. 4. Diese Stellung als Sekretärin ist gut bezahlt, warum bewirbst du dich nicht? 5. Fred Greens Sohn will nicht Dockarbeiter werden. 6. Er möchte Physiker werden.

5. Translate

1. Viele Leute nehmen drei Mahlzeiten am Tag [ein]. 2. Die Taylors gehen einmal im Jahr auf *(on)* Urlaub. 3. Diese Tomaten kosten 30p das Pfund. 4. Wieviele Zigaretten rauchen Sie pro Tag? 5. Diese Stenotypistin verdient weniger als 20 Pfund in der Woche, aber sie geht dreimal im Jahr in Urlaub. 6. Diese Zigaretten kosten 25p das Päckchen.

30 The Open Window

1. Fill in the right words

across, appeared, beyond, bodies, discomfort, fixed, funny, ghost, guns, hobby, illness, jokes, library, meanwhile, prospects, shooting, turned, very, warning, wet, why

"My aunt will be back in a few minutes, Mr Nuttle," said a young lady of sixteen. "(1) ..., perhaps you would like to take off your coat." He followed the girl into the (2) ...

"Poor Aunt! Her (3) … began three years ago on this (4) … day," said the girl. "You may wonder why we keep that French window open on this (5) … October afternoon. Out through that window, three years ago, her husband and two young brothers of his went off to go (6) … They never came back. Their (7) … were never found. Poor Aunt always thinks they will come back. That is (8) … that window is kept open."

At that moment the aunt (9) … To Nuttle's (10) … she talked all the time of the shooting (11) … for the winter and all the time her eyes were (12) … on the window and the wood (13) …

"Here they are at last," she cried. Nuttle (14) … in his seat. In the darkness three figures were walking (15) … the garden towards the window. They carried (16) … under their arms. Nuttle quickly took his hat and coat and, without (17) … he was through the hall and the front garden.

"Who was that (18) … man?" asked Mr Sappleton. "A Mr Nuttle," said his wife. "One might think he had seen a (19) …" The niece said nothing. (20) … of that kind were a (21) … of hers.

2. Fill in the right pronouns: *mine, yours, his, hers, ours*

Customs Officer: Are these suitcases (1) …, Madam?

Young Lady: These two are (2) …

Customs Officer: What about the third suitcase. Isn't it (3) …?

Young Lady: No, it isn't (4) … It belongs to my boy-friend.

Customs Officer: Why isn't he here to open it if it's (5) …?

Young Lady: He's taking an old lady to the boat-train. He's left his luggage here, because he's carrying (6) …

Customs Officer: I see. Quite a gentleman! His suitcase will have to stay here until I've examined its contents. You can take (7) … to the boat train. Tell your friend to come and open (8) …

(The young lady takes her two suitcases and leaves the customs hall. At the boat train her boy-friend is waiting for her.)

Young Man: Did you get our two suitcases with the silver through? You're sure you didn't make a mistake? These are (9) ... with the silver, aren't they?

Young Lady: These are (10) ... with the silver all right. Everything went exactly as we planned. I said that the third suitcase was (11) ... The customs officer wants to see what's in it. He's waiting for you. *(Both laugh and the young man hurries back to the customs hall.)*

3. Translate

Unterhaltung auf der Straße

Brown: Darf ich einen deutschen Freund von mir vorstellen? Heinz Schmidt aus Hamburg. Dies ist Bill Taylor, ein Nachbar von uns.

Taylor und Heinz Schmidt: Guten Tag!

Brown (zu Taylor): Gehört der neue Wagen vor deinem Haus dir?

Taylor: Nein, er gehört meiner Frau. Ich habe keinen eigenen Wagen. Haben Sie einen eigenen Wagen, Herr Schmidt?

Schmidt: Ja, ich habe einen eigenen Wagen in Deutschland.

Brown (zu Taylor): Ist deine Frau zu Hause?

Taylor: Nein, sie ist beim Friseur, wie gewöhnlich. Sind sie verheiratet, Herr Schmidt?

Schmidt: Meine Frau ist bei ihren Eltern in Deutschland. Sie haben ein eigenes Haus auf dem Land. Eine Schwester meiner Frau ist auch dort.

Taylor: Sie haben ein Paket unter dem Arm. Ist das ein Geschenk für ihre Frau?

Schmidt: Nein, es ist ein Geschenk für meine Wirtin. Sie ist immer sehr nett zu mir.

31 Don't

1. Fill in the right words

awake, bedtime, cough, custom, draughts, hand, pavement, polite, seated, shake, shovel, tip, unless

When you are in England:

DON'T drive on the right- (1) ... side of the road.

DON'T (2) ... hands, (3) ... you meet someone for the first time.

DON'T walk on the inside of the (4) ... when you are with a lady. If you did she would hardly think you very (5) ...
DON'T use your fork like a (6) ...
DON'T remain (7) ... in a restaurant when the lady leaves your table.
DON'T forget to leave a (8) ... on the table.
DON'T only pay for your own drink when you are in company. In England it is the (9) ... to order rounds.
DON'T refuse a cup of coffee at (10) ... English coffee won't keep you (11) ...
DON'T complain of (12) ... The English love fresh air and (13) ... a lot.

2. unless = if not

Example: You can't speak to a lady if you haven't been introduced to her.
You can't speak to a lady *unless you have* been introduced to her.

1. You'll never keep that position if you don't work harder. 2. If you don't stop these silly jokes, people won't ask you to visit them any more. 3. If you don't tell the police, you will never see your car again. 4. His wife wasn't happy if he didn't buy her expensive presents. 5. He's bad-tempered if he doesn't get what he wants. 6. They won't be able to buy a new house if they don't save. 7. I'll go to Italy next year if I don't go to Spain. 8. You'll never get better if you don't take your medicine regularly.

3. Short answers

a) *When Mr Nuttle came back to his boarding-house, he was still trembling with fright. His landlady tried to find out what had happened, but Mr Nuttle could only give short answers.*

Landlady	*Nuttle*
1. Did you see Mrs Sappleton?	(to do) Yes, I did.
2. Was she glad to see you?	(to think) I think so.
3. Her niece is a nice girl, isn't she?	(to suppose)
4. Is the girl intelligent?	(to believe)
5. Mrs Sappleton always has her windows open.	(to know)
6. Don't people catch colds easily at her place?	(to expect)

7. Are you all right? (to hope)

8. Would you like to have some whisky? (to think)

b) *The landlady wasn't very pleased with Nuttle's answers and continued with her questions. This time Nuttle gave negative (verneinte) short answers.*

Landlady	*Nuttle*
1. Did you have tea with Mrs Sappleton?	(to do) No, I didn't.
2. Will you go shooting tomorrow?	(to expect) I don't expect so.
3. Did you see Mr Sappleton?	(to know)
4. Did you meet Mrs Sappleton's brothers?	(to believe)
5. Will they call on you tonight?	(to hope)
6. Will you stay long in our village?	(to think)
7. Don't you like this place?	(to do)
8. Will you meet the Sappletons at the pub tonight?	(to suppose)

32 Stratford-on-Avon

1. Fill in the right words

age, anyone, dramatist, earth, famous, lasting, market, native, nature (2×), opportunities, outside, pleasant, poet, step

Shakespeare has made this town (1) ... Standing (2) ... the house where he was born in 1564, we hear most languages of the (3) ... and we see people of all nationalities, drawn here by the world's greatest (4) ...

Walking through the streets of this (5) ... little (6) ... town with its half-timbered houses, we are reminded at every (7) ... of the great (8) ...

At about the age of twenty-two Shakespeare went to London, the large city offering better (9) ... for an intelligent young man than a small town like Stratford. About 1610 Shakespeare returned to his (10) ... town, where he died six years later at the age of fifty-two. What is the secret of Shakespeare's (11) ... popularity after 360 years? Is it perhaps that Shakespeare, more than (12) ... else, understood the human heart and human (13) ..., and that human (14) ... does not change?

"He was not of an (15) ..., but for all time."

2. Shorten the sentences, using a participle

Example: Thousands of visitors, who wanted to see a Shakespeare play, had booked well in advance.
Thousands of visitors *wanting* to see a Shakespeare play had booked well in advance.

1. The Royal Shakespeare Theatre, which was showing "As You Like It" that afternoon, was booked to the last seat. 2. Visitors who wanted to eat and drink went to restaurants, pubs and snack-bars. 3. Others, who found Shakespeare's tombstone more interesting, went along the river to Holy Trinity Church. 4. The sunlight, which came through the church windows, shone on the tombstones of Shakespeare and his wife. 5. The Americans who go to see Anne Hathaway's cottage seem to be very pleased. 6. The schoolboy, who crept like a snail unwillingly to school, learnt little Latin and less Greek.

3. Shorten the sentences

Example: The tickets which were sold to us at the Royal Shakespeare Theatre were expensive.
The tickets *sold* to us at the Royal Shakespeare Theatre were expensive.

1. The garden which was shown to us had many beautiful flowers. 2. The epitaph which was engraved on Shakespeare's tombstone had been written by the poet himself. 3. The language which was taught at every grammar school in Shakespeare's England was Latin. 4. Women's parts *(Rollen),* which were played by boys, were often very difficult. 5. The twelve theatres, which were situated outside the city, had 2,000 seats each. 6. New Place, which was bought by Shakespeare, was the finest house in Stratford.

4. Connect the two sentences, using a participle

Example: The lady rose from her seat. She left the room quickly.
The lady rose from her seat, *leaving* the room quickly.

1. Millions of Londoners go to work in the City. They spend hours in trains, buses and the Underground. 2. Bill worked as a waiter. He earned £26 a week. 3. I walked

through the streets. I looked for a snack-bar. 4. "You mustn't expect fine food at a snack-bar," said my friend. He made a face. 5. "You may smoke in English cinemas," said my companion. He offered me a cigarette. 6. "Would you like to dance?" asked the man. He smiled at the woman in the blue dress.

5. Letter-writing

a) *Write a letter of introduction for your secretary, Miss Ingrid Steiner, to a business friend of yours. She is going to England to improve her English. You ask your business friend if he would be good enough to help her so that she won't feel lost in London. Begin like this:*

Dear Mr Gordon,

This is to introduce my secretary, Miss Ingrid Steiner, who is spending a holiday in London ...

Now give the following information about Miss Steiner:

1. Her age 2. Her London address 3. Where she learnt her English 4. What her hobbies are 5. What she would like to see in Britain 6. Ask where and how she could spend her evenings

Use one to three sentences connected with each of these six points. End the letter this way:

With kind regards, and thanking you in advance for your kind help,

Yours sincerely,

b) *Write Mr Gordon's answer to your letter, informing you that he met Miss Steiner in London.*

Mention the following points:

1. Where they met 2. What Miss Steiner is like 3. What Mr Gordon did to help her 4. Whether she has improved her English 5. What Miss Steiner likes most about England 6. What she doesn't like about England

Begin your letter like this:

Dear ...

Thank you for your letter of (date). I am pleased to inform you that ...

33 Starting a New Life in Australia

1. Fill in the right words

citizens, coast, crowded, emigrated, liner, map, noon, owned, ranged, referring, regretted, smoothly, soft, space, steadily, supplying

28-year-old Jane Bird was sitting in the bar on board the 30,000-ton ocean (1) … QUEEN OF AUSTRALIA.
"I'm going to open an ice-cream parlour in Sydney," she said, showing a (2) … of Sydney to the man who was sitting beside her. "In Victoria Street near the harbour."
Jane was (3) … to her business plans. Jane and George opened their ice-cream parlour in the first week of December. It was summer and temperatures (4) … from 32° to 36° centigrade at (5) … Soon they were (6) … their customers with ice-cream, Coca-Cola and other (7) … drinks as fast as they could fetch them out of the refrigerator.
Autumn came and lucky Jane and George already (8) … a chain of ice-cream parlours on the (9) … Their business went (10) … and grew (11) … They never (12) … that they had left old England with her awful weather and (13) … cities. They had (14) … to a country with sunshine and (15) … instead.
Being British, both George and Jane applied for registration as Australian (16) … one year after landing in Sydney.

2. With or without *the?*

Example: Drive carefully. *Life* is short, *death* is for ever.
The life which they led after *the death of* their father was hard.

1. … quality of the goods did not affect … quantity sold.
   … quality is more important than … quantity.
2. … love which she had felt for him had gone.
   … love has little to do with reason *(Vernunft)*.
3. … food is short in the Third World.
   … food we had eaten didn't agree with us.
4. When will you pay back … money I lent you?
   … money can't buy everything.

5. Nothing succeeds like … success.
   … success he has enjoyed in … life has made him very proud.
6. … progress of science is astonishing.
   The answer to the problem of hunger is … social progress.
7. … summer is the hottest season of the year.
   … summer of 1973 was specially hot in Spain.
8. … breakfast was always at 8 o'clock.
   We liked … breakfast she had prepared for us.

3. Translate

1. Der Hyde Park in London ist sonntags Spielplatz der Demokratie. 2. Die Toleranz ist dort zu Hause. 3. Die meisten Redner sprechen von *(of)* Fortschritt oder Politik. 4. Die meisten von ihnen glauben, daß sie die Welt verbessern können, aber das ist ein leerer Traum. 5. Andere sprechen von ihrer lieben alten Mutter, von der Qualität des Lebens, vom Tode und vom Teufel, vom Glück und vom Frieden. 6. Die meisten Menschen, die ihnen zuhören, lächeln und nehmen sie nicht ernst. 7. Die Rednerecke *(Speakers' Corner)* im Hyde Park gehört zu London genau wie die Oxford Street, die Tower Bridge und Victoria Station.

4. Letter-writing

Write a short letter applying for a £10 passage to Australia to the Chief Migration Officer (Haupteinwanderungsbeamter), Canberra House, London WC2. Give the following information:

1. Your full name and address 2. Your age 3. Nationality 4. Whether single or married 5. Number of children 6. Where you were educated 7. Occupation 8. Reasons why you want to emigrate to Australia

(Address)
(Date)

The Chief Migration Officer
Canberra House
London WC2

Dear Sir,

Refering to your advertisement in yesterday's Daily Mail, I should like to apply for …

Looking forward to an early reply,
Yours faithfully,
(signature)

Test III

1. Pronunciation

Find the same sound (Laut) **as that underlined in the sentence**

1. I w**ear** a different suit every second day.
   ☐ a) h**ear** ☐ b) ch**air** ☐ c) cl**er**k ☐ d) car**eer**
2. Two thirds of the world's population haven't en**ough** to eat.
   ☐ a) thr**ough** ☐ b) th**ough**t ☐ c) d**ou**bt ☐ d) r**ough**
3. Many students took the ox for a c**ow**.
   ☐ a) b**ow**l ☐ b) all**ow** ☐ c) fell**ow** ☐ d) gr**ow**
4. Do you remember the h**eight** of the World Trade Center in New York?
   ☐ a) w**eight** ☐ b) str**aight** ☐ c) g**ate** ☐ d) fl**ight**
5. Two policemen stopp**ed** him.
   ☐ a) tri**ed** ☐ b) climb**ed** ☐ c) look**ed** ☐ d) start**ed**

2. Stress

Underline the syllable (Silbe) **which has the main stress** (Hauptakzent)

Example: He came *immediately*.
im/**me**/diate/ly

1. Nigeria is a member of the *Commonwealth.* Com/mon/wealth
2. Britain belongs to the European *Community.* Com/mu/ni/ty
3. She is quite an *ordinary* girl. or/di/na/ry
4. Their car was *orange-coloured.* or/ange/col/oured
5. On Sundays Hyde Park is the playground of *democracy.* de/moc/ra/cy

3. Structures

Mark the correct answer with a cross ☒

1. When in England you ... drive on the right, but you ... have a driving licence.
   ☐ a) must – mustn't ☐ c) mustn't – must
   ☐ b) needn't – must ☐ d) mustn't – needn't

2. If you behave better, you ... feel happier.

☐ a) will ☐ c) can
☐ b) would ☐ d) must

3. If you ... a cup of coffee at bedtime, it wouldn't keep you awake.

☐ a) drink ☐ c) will
☐ b) would drink ☐ d) drank

4. If the service ... included, you won't have to leave a tip.

☐ a) is ☐ c) was
☐ b) were ☐ d) will be

5. She hasn't got ...

☐ a) an own flat, has she? ☐ c) a flat of her own, has she?
☐ b) a flat of hers, hasn't she? ☐ d) a flat of her own, hasn't she?

6. She is an aunt ...

☐ a) of him, isn't she? ☐ c) of his, is she?
☐ b) from him, isn't she? ☐ d) of his, isn't she?

7. There's nothing ... gives him any pleasure.

☐ a) whom ☐ c) who
☐ b) what ☐ d) that

8. Something ... reminded me of Germany.

☐ a) what she said ☐ c) of what she said
☐ b) which she said ☐ d) she said

9. The gentleman ... at the station ... of my brother.

☐ a) whom we met – remembered me ☐ c) we met – remembered me
☐ b) which we met – reminded me ☐ d) we met – reminded me

10. May we ...

☐ a) introduce? ☐ c) introduce ourself?
☐ b) ourselves introduce? ☐ d) introduce ourselves?

11. As I was ... I ... from the table.

☐ a) ashamed of myself – rose myself ☐ c) ashamed of me – rose myself
☐ b) ashamed of me – rose ☐ d) ashamed of myself – rose

12. Rhona applied … a job with Webber & Co.

☐ a) about ☐ b) because of ☐ c) for ☐ d) to

13. The staff manager was sitting … his desk.

☐ a) before ☐ b) behind ☐ c) beyond ☐ d) in front

14. I always set my watch … the radio.

☐ a) by ☐ b) at ☐ c) after ☐ d) with

15. We were given a room … the back.

☐ a) to ☐ b) on ☐ c) of ☐ d) at

4. Comprehension

Mark the best answer with a cross ☒

1. Has your horse lost in the Derby?

☐ a) I don't hope so. ☐ c) I hope it not.

☐ b) I don't hope it. ☐ d) I hope not.

2. Will your husband buy you a present for Christmas?

☐ a) I believe. ☐ c) I hope so.

☐ b) I think it. ☐ d) I suppose.

3. Will the plane take off in time?

☐ a) I don't know. ☐ c) I don't know it.

☐ b) I know not. ☐ d) I can't know.

4. Did you remember your wife's birthday?

☐ a) I forgot. ☐ c) I forgot so.

☐ b) No, I forgot it. ☐ d) No, I've forgotten it.

5. Did you catch your train?

☐ a) No, I lost it. ☐ c) No, I missed it.

☐ b) Yes, I caught. ☐ d) I missed.

34 The Boat Race

1. Fill in the right words

back, beaten, coach, foot, help, launch, mad, meeting, over, sense, strong, through, trouble, use, yet

"There, old boy, this time you're (1) ...," John announced to his American friend Joe. Joe had to admit that the crowds watching the Boat Race between the Universities of Oxford and Cambridge were bigger than any mass (2) ... in the States. "It's no (3) ... saying I enjoyed watching it," Joe continued, "for I did not. This morning I drove to Hammersmith. The weather was wet and cold, and (4) ..., by car, by (5) ..., on bicycles and on (6) ..., people were moving in one direction: to the river. Somebody suggested going on a (7) ... I got cold and wet (8) ... What was the (9) ... in that? And then they came. Eight (10) ... young men with a small shouting passenger at the (11) ... were rowing like (12) ... as if the devil were behind them. All I could see was (13) ... in about three minutes. I can't (14) ... thinking that I could have saved myself the (15) ..."

2. A telephone conversation

Use the gerund in the answers
Example: A: Why do you always *phone* when there is a film on TV?
B: Phoning is my hobby.

A: Why don't you *watch* television yourself?
B: (1) ... television is not very interesting.
A: Do you prefer to *go* to the theatre?
B: (2) ... to the theatre is even less entertaining.
A: Why don't you *learn* a foreign language?
B: (3) ... a foreign language is too difficult.
A: Why don't you *play* cards?
B: (4) ... cards is boring.
A: Don't you ever *cook* a nice meal for yourself?
B: (5) ... is something that women enjoy.
A: If I were you I'd *drink* a bottle of whisky to forget my troubles.

B: (6) ... whisky is bad for my health.

A: Can't you find anything better to do than to *phone* other people?

B: I already told you, (7) ... is my hobby.

3. Form sentences, using the gerund

Example: He/to suggest/to go to Stratford for the afternoon performance
He suggested *going* to Stratford for the afternoon performance.

1. He/to suggest/to go by car 2. She/to object to/to go by car 3. She/to love/to travel by train 4. She/to hate/to drive on crowded roads 5. He/to like/to drive at top speed 6. He/to suggest/to go by coach 7. She/not to like/to travel by coach 8. He/to give up/to suggest anything 9. She/to keep/to tell him that it was quicker by rail 10. He/to remember/to have seen "As You Like It" before 11. She/not to mind/to see it twice 12. As she/to prefer/to travel by train, he suggested the train for her and the car for himself

4. Put in the right prepositions: *in, of, on, to*

A: Well, I'm looking forward (1) ... having my first good meal in New York.

B: People have some difficulty (2) ... finding this restaurant, I believe.

A: Oh, do they? But I'm used (3) ... looking for places when I travel abroad. I always take the opportunity (4) ... going to a good restaurant.

B: I would never have succeeded (5) ... finding it without your help.

A: Shall we take the opportunity (6) ... ordering a bottle of good French wine?

B: I object (7) ... drinking any kind of alcohol. Besides, as I'm not accustomed (8) ... drinking wine, I'm afraid (9) ... making a fool of myself.

A: Good wine is completely harmless *(harmlos)*. Anyway, I wouldn't say no (10) ... having the best part *(Anteil)* of the bottle myself.

B: All right then! But I insist (11) ... paying the bill.

5. Translate

Nur eine Tasse Tee

1. „Ich bestehe darauf, die Post *(mail)* vor 10 Uhr zu bekommen", schrie der

Generaldirektor. 2. „Es hat keinen Zweck, sie später zu bekommen. 3. Ich muß Gelegenheit haben, die Post zu lesen, bevor ich beginne, Briefe zu diktieren. 4. Würde es Ihnen etwas ausmachen, in Zukunft darauf zu achten *(to see to it)?*“ 5. Rhona konnte nicht umhin zu lächeln, denn ihr Chef war nie im Büro vor 10 Uhr. 6. Sie war gewohnt, ihm die Post mit einer Tasse Tee zu bringen. 7. [An] jenem Tage gab es keine Aussicht *(chance),* Tee zu machen, weil die Gasarbeiter *(gas workers)* streikten. 8. Dies war der Grund, warum Rhona ihrem Chef die Post ohne die übliche *(usual)* Tasse Tee brachte. 9. Sie wußte, wie versessen *(keen)* ihr Chef darauf war, seinen Tee zu bekommen. 10. Sie konnte sich nicht erinnern, ihren Chef so böse gesehen zu haben. 11. Sie hatte Schwierigkeiten *(difficulty),* ein ernstes Gesicht zu bewahren *(to keep).* 12. „In solchem Maße kann eine kleine Tasse Tee die menschliche Natur verwandeln“, dachte sie.

35 Sales Psychology

1. Fill in the right words

addition, any, apply, arranging, block, by, charge, condition, draw, employers, extremely, far, fast, generous, grateful, partly, proves, reach, responsibility, shelf, slow

Dear Sirs,

On starting as a branch manager in the Dover supermarket I soon began to (1) ... some methods which increased sales (2) ... 20 per cent.

This increase was (3) ... realized by (4) ... the articles on show differently. (5) ... sellers like sugar and salt were within easy (6) ... of the public. That was wrong. Why (7) ... valuable space on the (8) ... with goods people will buy in (9) ... case? So I put the (10) ... sellers like toothbrushes, combs, lipsticks and powder in places where our female customers could not avoid seeing them.

As (11) ... as prices are concerned, it's just as bad to (12) ... too little as too much. Recently we had some apples. They were still in good (13) ..., but (14) ... ripe. So we were offering them at a very (15) ... price. "Must be something wrong with them," said a woman to her friend. The next day I put the price up, and all the apples were sold by the afternoon.

In writing this I wish to (16) ... your attention as my (17) ... to the fact that much of the success of a business depends on the skill and (18) ... of the branch manager. Yet, for three years I haven't had a rise in salary, which (19) ... that a good salesman has to sell not only goods to his customers but, in (20) ..., his ability to his employers.

I would be (21) ... if you would give this letter your close attention.

Yours faithfully,

John Smith

2. Das Gerundium mit eigenem Satzgegenstand

Bezieht sich das Gerundium nicht auf den Satzgegenstand des Hauptsatzes, so muß der neue Satzgegenstand vor das Gerundium gestellt werden. Bei Fürwörtern in Form des besitzanzeigenden Fürworts oder des persönlichen Fürworts wird:

I	zu	*my*	oder	*me*
you	zu	*your*	oder	*you*
he	zu	*his*	oder	*him*
it	zu	*its*	oder	*it*
we	zu	*our*	oder	*us*
they	zu	*their*	oder	*them*

Example: Do you mind *the boy* buying cigarettes?
Do you mind *his* buying cigarettes?
Do you mind *him* buying cigarettes?

1. Mrs Brown objects to her husband/to buy unnecessary things
2. She doesn't like her husband/to go to the supermarket alone
3. She doesn't mind her husband/to buy things when she is there
4. She insists on her children/to buy sweets with their own pocket money
5. "It's no use people/to say that children should have what they want"
6. She is keen on her daughter/to save money
7. She always complains of closing time/to be so early
8. Do you mind/I/to suggest some improvements?

3. Opposites

Use *un-, im-,* or *-less* for the missing words, which are opposites to the adjectives in the first part of the sentences.

Note that in the sentences below an adjective beginning with a *p* needs *im-* to form the opposite, an adjective ending with *-ful* takes *-less* to form the opposite, while all the others in the sentences below form their opposites with *un-*.

Example: pure – *im*pure; hope*ful* – hope*less;* necessary – *un*necessary

1. Though always trying to be *polite,* he often couldn't help being ... 2. Though she ought to have been *ashamed* of herself, she was quite ... 3. Although John Baker is an *educated* man, there are still many ... Negroes. 4. She remained quite *cheerful,* in spite of living in a ... room. 5. She gave him a *meaningful* look. To him it was ... 6. Although I'm *well* again, I was ... for quite a time. 7. He was *married,* but his sister remained ... 8. Be *careful* when driving a car as so many people are very ... in the street. 9. That State has a *powerful* government, its people are ... 10. As bad weather is *probable,* long hours of sunshine seem quite ... 11. How do you explain the fact that *intelligent* men so often marry ... women? 12. Though she was usually *willing* to work, that Monday morning she was ... to get up. 13. *Useful* things may be ugly, ... things may be beautiful. 14. Even in a *comfortable* bed, he feels ... in a hotel bedroom. 15. Though trying hard to be a *perfect* [ˈpəːfikt] housewife, she was ... in many ways.

4. Translate

1. Das Problem der Automation ist ernst *(a serious one).* 2. Eine Maschine tut die Arbeit von vielen Menschen. 3. Muß eine solche Entwicklung Arbeitslosigkeit verursachen? 4. Es ist eine Tatsache, daß Millionen von Menschen neue Stellungen *(jobs)* suchen müssen. 5. Viele Männer und Frauen wechseln ihre Berufe *(professions)* mehr als einmal in ihrem Leben (!). 6. Sie werden umgeschult. 7. Die Folgen einer solchen Entwicklung müssen sorgfältig studiert werden. 8. Könnte die 32-Stunden-Woche die Antwort sein? 9. Arbeitgeber, Gewerkschaften und der Staat werden das Problem lösen müssen. 10. In den USA, wo die Automation am meisten entwickelt ist, ist Arbeitslosigkeit ein großes Problem.

36

36 For Whites Only? I

1. Fill in the right words

anyone, approached, coloured, half, have, force, lazy, meet, middle (2×), movement, part, peace, protests, settle, slightest, under

Mrs Parks was a (1) ... woman, a widow of about fifty. She was waiting at the bus stop. When the bus came that late December afternoon, Mrs Parks got on it as she had done so many times before. One (2) ... of the bus – from the front to the (3) ... – was reserved for white people. From the (4) ... to the back the Negroes could sit. Mrs Parks was in the first seat behind the white (5) ... Shortly after Mrs Parks had sat down, the white bus driver (6) ... her. "We can't (7) ... Niggers sitting while Whites are standing," he said to her and three other Negroes. "Don't be (8) ... Get up at once." "I won't get up for (9) ...," she said. "I know my rights." "We'll soon (10) ... that," said the driver. "I'm not going to argue." He left the bus and returned to the scene with a policeman. "You ought to know better at your age," said the policeman. "Come on, you're (11) ... arrest for disturbing the (12) ..." In spite of her (13) ..., Mrs Parks was led away by (14) ... Rosa Parks had not the (15) ... idea that her refusal to (16) ... the bus driver's demand was the beginning of a nation-wide Negro (17) ... for freedom and black power.

2. much – many – a lot (of) – plenty (of)

a) *Example:* I haven't got ... English books, but I've got ... English records.
I haven't got *many* English books, but I've got *a lot of* English records.

1. My father doesn't drink ..., but he smokes ... 2. A journey to London doesn't cost as ... as a flight to New York, but it still costs ... 3. He doesn't talk ..., but when he does it's ... nonsense. 4. This town doesn't get ... sunshine, but it gets ... of rain. 5. How ... dresses will she take with her? ...! Two for every day of the week. 6. She doesn't swim ..., but she plays ... tennis. 7. Were there ... people at the meeting? Yes, ... people listened to his speech. 8. You don't make ... mistakes when you write, but when you speak you make ...

b) *Example:* You've done ... work this afternoon, but you didn't work ... yesterday.
You've done *a lot of* work this afternoon, but you didn't work *much* yesterday.

1. He's got ... money, but he doesn't spend ... on cars. 2. There was ... room in the train, but not ... people found seats in the dining-car. 3. We'll have ... time if we go by car, but we mustn't drink ... beer on the way. 4. She has seen ... London, though she didn't have ... time. 5. Englishmen spend ... time in pubs. Do ... Germans do the same? 6. We took ... pictures of the Lake District, but not ... were really good.

3. Fill in: *some, somebody (someone), something, any, anybody (anyone), anything*

1. If ... deserved to have a seat that December afternoon in 1955, it was Mrs Parks. 2. She had been waiting at the bus stop with ... other people. 3. When Mrs Parks entered the Negro part of the bus, there were still ... seats unoccupied. 4. ... minutes later, however, they were all filled and ... black and white people were standing. 5. The bus driver told her to give up her seat for ... else. 6. Mrs Parks said there wasn't ... in the world who could force her to get up. 7. "If ... else wants to get up, let him do so," she said, "but I'm not." 8. ... white man said ... about 'impossible behaviour', and the bus driver went to fetch a policeman. 9. "I wouldn't have said ... if there had been ... seats left," said the bus driver to the policeman. "But as you can see there aren't ..." 10. "If there's ... that makes my blood boil," said the policeman, "it's a Negro disturbing the peace. ... is wrong in a country where this can happen." 11. ... people laughed as they saw Mrs Parks being led away. 12. There wasn't ... among them who realized that this was the beginning of a nation-wide Negro movement for freedom.

4. Fill in: *another (4×), different (4×), other (1×), somebody (1×), something (1×)*

1st stewardess: When I marry I'll have to look for (1) ... job. You can't be a stewardess and a housewife at the same time.

2nd stewardess: A job in an office is very (2) ... from your work on a plane. Will you give up flying immediately?

1st stewardess: I don't think so. I might go on with this job for (3) ... six months. Then I'll look for (4) ... else.

2nd stewardess: (5) ... job won't be so interesting, will it? On each (6) ... flight we meet (7) ... people. Would you like (8) ... cup of tea?

1st stewardess: Yes, please. I don't think life will be very (9) ... for you. As soon as I leave, (10) ... else will step in and do my work. I don't see any (11) ... way.

5. Translate the sentences below into German, always using 'man'

1. You can't be a stewardess and a housewife at the same time. 2. People shouldn't say such things. 3. One doesn't do that sort of thing. 4. He wasn't trusted. 5. On Saturday afternoons we can watch them play football. 6. One never can tell. 7. The dog was heard barking all night. 8. You can't always believe what people say.

6. Translate

1. Die Welternährungskrise wird in den Vereinigten Staaten von jeder Hausfrau gespürt. 2. In *(On)* den Nachrichten hört man nichts als *(but)* Berichte *(reports)* über die hohen Rindfleischpreise. 3. Die Regierung hoffte, daß ein Preisstop für *(on)* Rindfleisch das Problem lösen würde. 4. Der Preisstop half nicht viel. 5. Das Fleisch verschwand und wenn jemand ein Steak haben wollte, mußte es auf dem schwarzen Markt gekauft werden. 6. Gibt es irgendwelche Gründe für die Fleischknappheit *(scarcity* ['skɛəsiti]) in den Staaten? 7. Einige Leute behaupten *(maintain),* daß Japan [dʒə'pæn] zu viel Fleisch in Amerika kauft. 8. Früher aßen *(used to eat)* die Japaner *(Japanese* [ˌdʒæpə'ni:z]) mehr Fisch als irgendeine andere Nation in der Welt. 9. Heute importieren sie *(to import)* siebenmal soviel Rindfleisch aus Amerika wie vor zehn Jahren, fünfzehnmal soviel Wein aus Europa *(Europe* ['juərəp]), und zwanzigmal soviel Hammelfleisch aus Australien. 10. Sie bezahlen gut, denn sie verdienen viel. 11. Ist es [dann] erstaunlich, daß die Steaks in Amerika, die europäischen Weine und das australische Hammelfleisch teurer werden? 12. 110 Millionen Japaner sind gute Kunden für Fleisch. Es ist eine Frage von Angebot und Nachfrage.

37 For Whites Only? II

1. Fill in the right words

action, blamed, case, driving, favour, fired, hired, holding, ideals, in, minister, organize, quarters, racial, reacted, struggle, task, victory, wherever

Twenty-four hours after Mrs Parks' arrest, the Negro leaders were (1) … a meeting to discuss a plan of (2) …
It was decided to (3) … a bus boycott for the following Monday. A young Baptist (4) …, Dr Martin Luther King, took on the (5) … of spreading the news to Montgomery's 50,000 Negro citizens.
On Monday morning the buses driving through the Negro (6) … were empty. The Whites (7) … sharply. They (8) … King together with other Negro leaders for the boycott, and put them in prison. But this time the Negroes would not give (9) …
The (10) … was taken to the United States Supreme Court which decided in (11) … of the Negroes. From then on they were allowed to sit or stand in buses (12) … there was room. The Negro movement had won its first (13) … King became the (14) … force of the movement.
Many young Negroes, however, have not accepted King's (15) … Their anger is largely caused by unemployment. Often they are the last (16) … and the first (17) … Can the USA find an answer to its Negro problem – a problem which is both social and (18) …? The (19) … goes on.

2. for or since?

A: Rosa Parks has been in prison (1) … five days.
B: Yes, she's been there (2) … last Friday.
A: (3) … when have you known of her arrest?
B: (4) … King spread the idea of the bus boycott.
A: The bus boycott will last (5) … quite a time.
B: King has been under arrest (6) … yesterday.
A: I'm not surprised. I've expected that (7) … a long time.
B: (8) … many years we've shown amazing patience. We've suffered because of our colour ever (9) … we were born. Now our patience has come to an end.

3. Rosa Parks

Example: Do you know Rosa Parks? (50 years/she was a baby)
I've known her for 50 years.
I've known her *since* she was a baby.

1. Does she work at the High Street Department Store? (15 years/1940) 2. Is she a widow? (quite a time/the end of the war) 3. Is she a Baptist? (30 years/she was twenty) 4. Does she live in Montgomery? (a long time/Easter 1935) 5. Do you know her brother John? (some months/August) 6. Does he know she's in prison? (some days/her arrest)

4. Translate

Use the past tense in all the sentences

Aus *(From)* einem Brief eines Montgomery Negers

1. Du möchtest wissen, was ich gestern getan habe. 2. Nun, ich bin in der Baptistenkirche gewesen und habe Martin Luther King zugehört. 3. Unser Vater, der vor zwei Jahren gestorben ist, wäre sehr glücklich gewesen *(would have been)*, wenn er diese Rede gehört hätte. 4. Hast du nicht unsere Versammlung gestern abend im *(on)* Fernsehen gesehen? 5. Die Presse *(press)* hat eine Menge Fotos [auf]genommen. 6. Der vergangene *(last)* Sonntag ist ein großer Tag gewesen. 7. Die Verhaftung von Rosa Parks vor drei Tagen ist das Ereignis gewesen, das zur Gleichberechtigung *(equal rights)* führen könnte *(might)*.

5. Translate

Am Telefon

A: Haben Sie unser Angebot [schon] bekommen?

B: Ja, es ist vor drei Tagen angekommen. Haben Sie [schon] die Muster geschickt?

A: Wir haben Ihnen die Muster am Montag zugesandt.

B: Sie sind noch nicht angekommen. Wir müssen die Muster sehen, bevor wir Ihnen den Auftrag geben.

A: Wir verkaufen diese Ware seit Jahren.

B: Was sind Ihre Zahlungsbedingungen?

A: Bar ohne Abzug binnen 30 Tagen nach Rechnungsdatum.

B: Ich hoffe, wir werden zu einer Einigung kommen. Danke für den Anruf *(call).*

38 London Through the Ages

1. Fill in the right words

busiest, centre, commerce, exports, half-way, keep, local, meet, population, protected, queue, striking, suburbs, temper, thirsty, was

Although London was already a town in the days of the Romans, it (1) ... not to become the capital of England until the 12th century. In Shakespeare's age there were two different cities a few miles apart from each other. One was the City of London (2) ... by its grey walls, the other, the royal City of Westminster, where Parliament used to (3) ... People going from Westminster to London would pass green fields and, perhaps, stop (4) ... at the village of Charing Cross for a drink when they were (5) ...
Today Charing Cross is one of the (6) ... parts of this strange mixture of old and new called Greater London, which has a (7) ... of 7 million.
London is not only the (8) ... of the nation's (9) ... and trade, but also the biggest industrial town in England and the largest port. 39 per cent of Britain's (10) ... are sent from the Port of London. Millions of Londoners will spend hours daily in (11) ... trains, buses and the Underground, taking them from the (12) ... into town and back again. Though everyone wants to get home as quickly as possible in the evening, they will still (13) ... order and discipline. No one will get out of a (14) ..., nor will anyone lose his (15) ... This disciplined behaviour is one of London's most (16) ... features.

2. to be to

a) „sollte" im Sinne von „das Schicksal wollte es"

Translate: 1. Der kleine Hafen an *(on)* der Themse sollte eine der größten Städte der Welt werden. 2. Die frühere Hauptstadt, Winchester, sollte ein unbedeutendes Marktstädtchen werden. 3. Das Dorf Charing Cross sollte eines der Zentren von

London werden. 4. In [der] Westminster Abtei sollten die meisten englischen Dichter eine Ruhestätte *(place of rest)* finden. 5. Shakespeare sollte nicht in [der] Westminster Abtei begraben werden. 6. Er sollte in Stratford, seinem Geburtsort, liegen.

b) „sollen" im Sinne einer strengen Anweisung

1. Stop that game at once. 2. Don't smoke during lessons. 3. Father says you mustn't meet that man again. 4. Members of the staff are forbidden to have private phone calls during office hours. 5. You must do the work I give you. 6. Must we wait for a rise in salary until next year?

Use *to be to* in all the sentences above

1. You are to stop that game at once. (go on)

3. A disappointing holiday

Your friend spent a holiday at Brighton, but he did not enjoy himself for various reasons.

a) *Example: A:* He stayed at an expensive hotel and spent too much money.
B: He shouldn't have stayed at an expensive hotel.

1. *A:* He went there in August when the beach was crowded.
   B: He ...
2. *A:* He lay in the sun so long that he got a bad headache.
   B: He ...
3. *A:* He bathed in the sea after lunch and felt sick.
   B: He ...
4. *A:* He ate a lot of ice-cream and made himself ill.
   B: He ...
5. *A:* He walked on the beach without his shoes on and cut his foot on a piece of glass.
   B: He ...
6. *A:* He drove a car when he had drunk too much beer.
   B: He ...

b) Now give B's answers, using *he ought to*

Example: A: He stayed at an expensive hotel and spent a lot of money. (to stay at a guest-house)
B: He ought to have stayed at a guest-house.

1. *B:* (June or September)
2. *B:* (in the shade)
3. *B:* (to wait at least two hours after lunch)
4. *B:* (to eat sandwiches instead)
5. *B:* (to wear tennis shoes)
6. *B:* (to take a taxi)

4. Conversation on board the QUEEN OF AUSTRALIA

a) Add short answers with *so*
Example: Jane: I enjoy life on board. (I)
George: So do I.

1. I sold everything I had before leaving England. (I) 2. My mother cried when I said good-bye. (mine) 3. My brother took me to Southampton by car. (mine) 4. I was rather sad the first day on board. (I) 5. I would have returned home if I had been able to. (I) 6. After some days I got accustomed to life on board. (I) 7. I enjoy the food, the fresh air, in fact everything. (all the emigrants) 8. I'm looking forward to starting a new life in Australia. (most people on board) 9. I've heard that Australia is one of the richest countries in the world. (I) 10. My family will follow me as soon as possible. (mine)

b) Now give George's answers in this way:
Example: Jane: I enjoy life on board. (I)
George: I do, too.

c) Add short answers with *neither* or *nor*
Example: Jane: I haven't written to my family yet. (I)
George: Nor (neither) have I.

1. I haven't booked a hotel room in Sydney yet. (I) 2. I can't understand why so many people take the plane to Australia. (I) 3. Many people won't have a holiday for years after landing. (I) 4. However, I don't always enjoy life on board. (I) 5. My neighbours on board aren't very quiet. (mine) 6. Their children don't go to bed early enough. (my neighbours' children) 7. I didn't want to complain to the captain. (I) 8. But I can't allow such behaviour any longer. (other people) 9. The captain hasn't shown himself for days. (his officers) 10. Not many children know what discipline really is. (adults)

d) Now give George's answers in this way:

Example: Jane: I haven't written to my family yet. (I)
George: I haven't either.

39 The Channel Tunnel

1. Fill in the right words

ahead, according, bound, calculated, carried, considerable, difficulty, economic, engineering, every, exchange, hesitation, politicians, put, reality, shares, supported

For more than 170 years building a tunnel under the English Channel has been dreamt of by engineers and (1) ... At last an end has been (2) ... to fears and (3) ... The tunnel is about to become (4) ...
If everything goes (5) ... to plan, travellers will be carried by trains under the Channel as easily as they now travel by Underground under the Thames. The trains will run (6) ... five minutes. The (7) ... advantages are believed to be (8) ... Freight costs are (9) ... to be half as high as they are today. The (10) ... of goods between Britain and the Continent is (11) ... to become cheaper. Considering all the advantages that are to be expected, it is surprising that Britain did not go (12) ... with the tunnel sooner, as it is a piece of (13) ... which can be (14) ... out without great (15) ... And yet, the tunnel project is not (16) ... in all British circles.
In spite of all the protests, the "Chunnel" (17) ... are rising.

2. A hotel manager gives advice to his staff

a) *Put into the passive voice*
Example: We must deal with the wishes of the visitors immediately.
The wishes of the visitors *must be dealt with* immediately.

1. We must never laugh at funny clothes or hats. 2. We must look after old people well. 3. We must take care of the tourists' baggage. 4. We must look upon each tourist as a very important person. 5. We must always listen to complaining customers. 6. We must respect the tourists' wishes. 7. We must take care of animals like dogs, cats and birds.

b) *Later an American tourist writes to his friend in America*
Example: The wishes of the visitors *were dealt with* immediately.

1. Funny clothes or hats were never ... (go on)

3. neither or none?

Beachte: *Neither* = keiner von zweien; *none* = keiner von mehreren

1. Dick and Mary are a young married couple. ... of them drives a car. 2. The police questioned the landlady and her daughters. ... of them knew Mr Bilk's new address. 3. Mr Jones's two sons attend a comprehensive school. ... of them has any difficulty at school. 4. Many people visit Stratford. ... are disappointed. 5. Ingrid and her French boy-friend loved one another. ... of them admitted it. 6. ... of the people we met at the garden party had been to Germany.

4. neither – not ... either

Example: Which of the two sisters do you like?
Neither of them. I *don't* like *either* of them.

1. Which of the two houses do you want to buy? 2. Which of the two typists will you engage? 3. Which of the two trips have you chosen? 4. Which of the two stories do you like? 5. Which of the two girls must we invite? 6. Which of the two jobs will you take?

40 North Sea Gas and Oil

1. Fill in the right words

areas, by, capital, discovery, doubted, eagerly, employment, extraordinary, fields, fishing, headquarters, likely, mines, natural, off (2×), plants, pollution, property, raw, riches, surface

At one time all that Britain got out of the North Sea was fish. Then, in 1964, (1) ... gas was discovered (2) ... the east coast. News to be received even more (3) ... was the (4) ... of oil (5) ... the Scottish coast in 1969. These oil (6) ... are believed to be large enough to supply such quantities of the valuable liquid that the whole of Britain is

(7) … to become independent of the oil (8) … under the desert (9) … of the Middle East (10) … the early 1990's.

The development of (11) … material in the North Sea demands (12) … efforts of organization and (13) … In Scotland, where unemployment was rather high in comparison to the south of England, (14) … figures have risen already. Lately, more than eighty companies have set up their (15) … in Aberdeen where (16) … prices in some (17) … have doubled in the last two years.

However, there are always two sides to a coin. (18) … and other local industries in the North are already anxious about the new development. There are fears of (19) … of both air and sea.

It is to be (20) … that North Sea oil reserves will last much longer than 30 years. To feed her industry with the necessary energy, Britain will either have to go back to her coal (21) … or she will have to develop her atomic (22) … further.

2. Preparing for a journey

Use the passive infinitive of the verb

Example: Quite a number of things have (to do)
Quite a number of things *have to be done.*

1. The suitcases have (to pack) 2. The cat has (to take) to the neighbours 3. Money is (to fetch) from the bank 4. Various bills are (to pay) 5. All the doors are (to lock) 6. Our holiday address is (to leave) with the neighbours

3. Use the infinitive instead of a relative clause (Beifügungssatz)

Example: Britain needs something that can give her independence from desert oil.
Britain needs *something to give* her independence from desert oil.

1. Britain is building a number of atomic plants which could increase the nation's energy reserves. 2. The reserves of natural gas which are found in the North Sea are very large. 3. Britain is not the only country in Europe that uses North Sea gas. 4. Britain's energy reserves have reached proportions which were not expected 10 years ago. 5. Twenty years ago coal was the chief raw material which supplied

European energy needs. 6. Today the world's industrial countries spend fortunes on desert oil which keeps their factories going.

4. Use the infinitive instead of a relative clause

Put the preposition after the verb
Example: Your room is something *of which you can be proud.*
Your room is something *to be proud of.*

A: I'm lonely here in London. I have nobody *to whom I can talk.*

B: Well, I can give you the address of a club *to which you can go.*

A: I'd like to know some young people *with whom I can dance* on Saturdays. I'm always in my room at weekends.

B: A room is something *in which you sleep,* not a place *in which you spend your weekends.*

A: Can't you give me some names of people *on whom I could call* at weekends?

B: The organization *to which you could apply* is the International Friendship League.

41 From Empire to Commonwealth I

1. Fill in the right words

altogether, attempts, balance, beginning, Crown, defeat, favoured, fleet, growth, link, loss, mother, policy, rule, setback, trading, unrest, well, wings

The victory of the English (1) … over the Spanish Armada in 1588 made England a sea-power. Now she was able to stretch her (2) … over the seas. A colony in North America and a (3) … company in India under Elizabeth I were the first (4) … to build an Empire. In the 17th century political as (5) … as religious reasons (6) … emigration to the east coast of North America.
The 18th century was (7) … marked by the English (8) … of maintaining the (9) … of power in Europe to prevent any country from becoming strong enough to be a danger to England.

The Empire reached the height of its power with the (10) … of the Boers in South Africa in 1902.

During this steady (11) … of their Empire, the British had suffered only one (12) …, but a very serious one: the (13) … of their North American colonies. This taught the English a lesson. When Canada showed signs of (14) … in the 19th century, the government granted home (15) … to this large country. The first British dominion was born. It was followed at the (16) … of the 20th century by Australia, New Zealand and the Union of South Africa. After the First World War these four dominions were granted complete independence. Together with the (17) … country they formed the British Commonwealth of Nations. Their common political (18) … was loyalty to the (19) …

2. Put in 'one' or 'ones' where necessary

1. Philip II (the second) was King of Spain and a very (powerful) at that. 2. As a young man he married an English Queen, Mary, but their marriage was not a (happy). 3. After Mary's death in 1558 another woman, a very (clever), became Queen of England. Her name was Elizabeth I (the first). 4. Though she was a Protestant, Philip wrote several letters to her, very (urgent), offering her his hand. 5. Elizabeth's answers were always (hesitating). 6. Meanwhile English sailors, especially (famous) like Drake and Hawkins, attacked the Spanish ships carrying gold and silver from South America. 7. Again and again Philip sent his protests, and we can imagine that he did not send (mild), to Elizabeth. 8. In spite of these, Drake continued to fill his pockets and those of his Queen with Spanish silver and gold, and it is known that Elizabeth's share was not a (small). 9. Finally, Philip of Spain lost patience and he built a fleet, a (large), which left Spain in 1588 with 30,000 soldiers on board. 10. This army, which was a very (strong), intended to land in England. 11. When the Spanish fleet entered the Channel, the English ships, (small) in comparison to the big (Spanish), started to attack. 12. It was impossible for the Spanish army to land in England. The English fleet had sunk a few ships when a terrible storm came up, a very (heavy), which destroyed quite a number of Spanish ships while the (English) sailed back to the safety of their ports.

3. Translate

Die Engländer

1. Man sagt, daß die Engländer sehr stolz darauf sind, englisch zu sein. 2. Wenn sie einen gut aussehenden *(good-looking)* Ausländer sehen, sagen sie: „Er sieht aus wie ein Engländer." 3. Viele Deutsche lernen Englisch, aber wenige Engländer lernen Deutsch. 4. Die Römer leben in Rom, die Schweizer in der Schweiz, die Spanier in Spanien, die Chinesen in China, aber die Engländer leben zu Hause. 5. Auf dem Schiff waren drei Franzosen, zwei Italienerinnen und drei Engländer. 6. Nur die Engländer sprachen nicht miteinander *(to each other)*, da sie nicht vorgestellt worden waren.

42 From Empire to Commonwealth II

1. Fill in the right words

admired, block, error, failed, frequently, gone, guide, independent (2×), majority, member, monarch, permitted, republic

After the Second World War, India was granted freedom within the British Commonwealth of Nations, the result being three (1) ... states, the Union of India, Pakistan and Ceylon. As the word 'British' only applied to white (2) ... states, this word was dropped and the name most (3) ... used today is 'The Commonwealth'. More and more parts of the Empire have been (4) ... to govern themselves since the last world war.

In 1957 the first African Negro colony became (5) ... under the name of Ghana. First recognizing the Queen as her (6) ..., Ghana, after three years, proclaimed herself a (7) ... within the Commonwealth. The countries with a coloured population already form the (8) ... in the Commonwealth. They all have economic and cultural links with Britain and they expect her to help but not (9) ... them in the future.

Meanwhile, members of the Commonwealth have even (10) ... to war with each other. Was the Commonwealth idea an (11) ...? Though the idea may have (12) ... to be the string holding the former Empire together in one (13) ..., the attempt in itself deserves to be (14) ...

2. to cause/to make (= veranlassen)

a) *Example:* They had to give up their plans because of bad weather.
Bad weather *caused them to give up* their plans.

1. The farmers had to stop work because of the floods. 2. The British looked for North Sea oil because of the world oil shortage. 3. Millions of fish died because of pollution. 4. We left our hotel because of the bad service. 5. Our boat was late because of fog over the Channel. 6. Britain gave up her Empire because of political and economic difficulties.

b) Now use *to make* for the sentences above

Example: Bad weather *made them give up* their plan.

3. Translate

1. Der zweite Weltkrieg veranlaßte die Engländer, ihr Weltreich aufzugeben. 2. Anstatt für ihre Kolonien zu kämpfen, wie [es] die Franzosen in Vietnam und Nordafrika taten, zwangen die Briten kein Land, Mitglied des Commonwealth zu bleiben. 3. Die Engländer machten einen großen Fehler, der sie ihre amerikanischen Kolonien verlieren ließ. 4. Sie lernten ihre Lektion. Als im 19. Jahrhundert Kanada Zeichen der Unruhe zeigte, gewährte Großbritannien dieser Kolonie Selbstverwaltung und später völlige Unabhängigkeit. 5. Mit dem Wechsel vom Weltreich zum Commonwealth ist eine neue Gemeinschaft von Nationen entstanden.

Test IV

1. Structures

Mark the correct answer with a cross ☒

1. Without ..., he ordered some expensive wine.
   - ☐ a) to know what he did
   - ☐ b) having known what he does
   - ☐ c) knowing what he does
   - ☐ d) knowing what he was doing

2. He was used to ... day and night.
   - ☐ a) work hard
   - ☐ b) working hard
   - ☐ c) have worked
   - ☐ d) have to work

3. At last I succeeded ... the exit.
   - ☐ a) to find
   - ☐ b) in finding
   - ☐ c) to finding
   - ☐ d) finding

4. You'll come to the party, too, ...?
   - ☐ a) do you
   - ☐ b) you will
   - ☐ c) don't you
   - ☐ d) won't you

5. He looked forward to ...
   - ☐ a) receiving a letter from her.
   - ☐ b) receive a letter from her.
   - ☐ c) having received a letter from her.
   - ☐ d) have received a letter from her.

6. He objected to ...
   - ☐ a) go to the office so early.
   - ☐ b) going to the office so early.
   - ☐ c) have gone to the office so early.
   - ☐ d) have to go to the office so early.

7. He succeeded ... the first prize.
   - ☐ a) to win
   - ☐ b) winning
   - ☐ c) of winning
   - ☐ d) in winning

8. We look forward ... you soon.
   - ☐ a) to see
   - ☐ b) to seeing
   - ☐ c) seeing
   - ☐ d) on seeing

9. I insist ... you home.
   - ☐ a) on taking
   - ☐ b) on bringing
   - ☐ c) taking
   - ☐ d) bringing

10. He didn't remember ... her before.
   - ☐ a) to have seen
   - ☐ b) having seen
   - ☐ c) to see
   - ☐ d) to seeing

11. Do you mind ... a little longer?
   - ☐ a) to wait
   - ☐ b) to be waiting
   - ☐ c) waiting
   - ☐ d) to have waited

12. Suddenly I heard ...
   - ☐ a) being called my name.
   - ☐ b) my name called.
   - ☐ c) calling my name.
   - ☐ d) my name call.

13. The two drivers lost ... in a crash.
   - ☐ a) their life
   - ☐ b) the lives
   - ☐ c) life
   - ☐ d) their lives

14. Does your friend enjoy ...
   - ☐ a) the life in the country?
   - ☐ b) life on the country?
   - ☐ c) life of the country?
   - ☐ d) life in the country?

15. I prefer ...
- ☐ a) English beer to the German wine.
- ☐ b) English beer to German wine.
- ☐ c) the English beer to German wine.
- ☐ d) the English beer to the German wine.

16. We saw the accident with ...
- ☐ a) my own eyes.
- ☐ b) the eyes of our own, didn't we?
- ☐ c) our own eyes, didn't we?
- ☐ d) our own eyes, haven't we?

17. John is a friend ...
- ☐ a) of you, isn't he?
- ☐ b) of your, is he?
- ☐ c) from you, isn't he?
- ☐ d) of yours, isn't he?

18. The gentleman ... yesterday was an American.
- ☐ a) we are waiting for at the airport
- ☐ b) who we're waiting for at the airport
- ☐ c) whom we were waiting on at the airport
- ☐ d) we were waiting for at the airport

19. John Baker, ... to serve people in a London hotel, became a professor of physics.
- ☐ a) the job of whom it was
- ☐ b) whose job it is
- ☐ c) whose job it was
- ☐ d) who had the job

20. Do you smoke? No, I don't. My brother doesn't smoke ...
- ☐ a) also.
- ☐ b) too.
- ☐ c) neither.
- ☐ d) either.

21. I went to the seaside two years ago ...
- ☐ a) So has my sister.
- ☐ b) So did my sister.
- ☐ c) So my sister did.
- ☐ d) So had my sister.

22. My mother won't buy her bacon at that shop any more. ... my wife.
- ☐ a) Also not
- ☐ b) Nor will
- ☐ c) Neither is
- ☐ d) Nor wants

23. Your luggage is very ...

- ☐ a) difficult.
- ☐ b) not light.
- ☐ c) heavy.
- ☐ d) easy.

24. When Rhona stepped ... the street, it was raining ...

- ☐ a) in – heavy.
- ☐ b) into – heavy.
- ☐ c) into – heavily.
- ☐ d) in – heavily.

25. The speaker said ... important.

- ☐ a) something
- ☐ b) everything
- ☐ c) some
- ☐ d) someone

26. ... he can do, his wife can do better.

- ☐ a) Anybody
- ☐ b) Anything
- ☐ c) Something
- ☐ d) All

27. We always ... to Wimbledon by bus.

- ☐ a) go
- ☐ b) drive
- ☐ c) roll
- ☐ d) run

28. He ... like an actor.

- ☐ a) sees
- ☐ b) remembers
- ☐ c) looks
- ☐ d) reminds

29. I have been living in England ...

- ☐ a) since two years.
- ☐ b) before two years.
- ☐ c) two years ago.
- ☐ d) for two years.

30. They disappeared three years ... on this very day.

- ☐ a) before
- ☐ b) since
- ☐ c) after
- ☐ d) ago

31. We ... married ... Christmas.

- ☐ a) have been – at
- ☐ b) are – since
- ☐ c) have been – since
- ☐ d) have been – before

32. The Dover supermarket ... last year.

- ☐ a) has opened
- ☐ b) has been opened
- ☐ c) opened
- ☐ d) has got opened

33. If my horse wins the Derby,
I ... buy a new car.
- ☐ a) am able
- ☐ b) am able to
- ☐ c) will be able
- ☐ d) will be able to

34. If we refused early morning tea,
our host ...
- ☐ a) will be astonished.
- ☐ b) would be astonished.
- ☐ c) will have been astonished.
- ☐ d) would have been astonished.

35. If we had flown to London we ...
- ☐ a) would have saved a lot of time.
- ☐ b) will have saved much time.
- ☐ c) would save a lot of time.
- ☐ d) would save much time.

36. I ... on the right-hand side of the shop.
- ☐ a) let the fast sellers place
- ☐ b) made the fast sellers placed
- ☐ c) got the fast sellers placing
- ☐ d) had the fast sellers placed

37. I can't read this letter. I ...
- ☐ a) must let it translated.
- ☐ b) must get it translate.
- ☐ c) must have it translated.
- ☐ d) let it translate.

38. I ... her for ten years.
- ☐ a) have known
- ☐ b) know
- ☐ c) am knowing
- ☐ d) do know

2. Comprehension

Mark the best explanation (Erklärung) **with a cross** ☒

1. Don't mention it.
- ☐ a) Thank you so much.
- ☐ b) That's all right.
- ☐ c) Please.
- ☐ d) It's nothing much.

2. What's the matter with him?
- ☐ a) Is he ill?
- ☐ b) What's wrong with him?
- ☐ c) What happened to him?
- ☐ d) He isn't in trouble, is he?

3. Can I call on you tomorrow?
- ☐ a) Can I ring you up tomorrow?
- ☐ b) May I visit you tomorrow?
- ☐ c) Will you be my guest tomorrow?
- ☐ d) Will you come if i call you tomorrow?

4. May I give you a lift?
- ☐ a) May I show you my car?
- ☐ b) Shall we take the lift?
- ☐ c) Shall I take you home?
- ☐ d) Would you like me to drive you somewhere?

5. Turn to the right.
- ☐ a) Take the first turning on the right.
- ☐ b) Keep to the right side of the road.
- ☐ c) Go right to the end of this road.
- ☐ d) Don't drive on the left-hand side.

6. It weighs heavily on my mind.
- ☐ a) It worries me.
- ☐ b) I'm sorry.
- ☐ c) The task is too much for me.
- ☐ d) I've got a lot of troubles.

7. This might apply to any kind of job.
- ☐ a) Some people apply for any kind of job.
- ☐ b) There are all kinds of applicants for a special kind of job.
- ☐ c) This might be true of all sorts of jobs.
- ☐ d) Any kind of job has its difficulties.

8. The case was closed for the police.
- ☐ a) The suitcase was locked so that the police should not open it.
- ☐ b) The police found out what had happened.
- ☐ c) The police had not been successful in their inquiries.
- ☐ d) The police did not need any more details.

9. He used to be a taxi driver.
- ☐ a) He was used as a taxi driver by his employers.
- ☐ b) He was usually a taxi driver.
- ☐ c) He once worked as a taxi driver.
- ☐ d) He was often a taxi driver.

10. A letter of introduction is ...
- ☐ a) the answer to an advertisement.
- ☐ b) a letter in which the visitor introduces himself.
- ☐ c) a letter asking for an interview.
- ☐ d) a letter in which a person is recommended to someone else.

Mark the best answer with a cross ☒

11. Do you mind if I smoke?
    - ☐ a) I hope not.
    - ☐ b) I don't think so.
    - ☐ c) Not at all.
    - ☐ d) Of course.

12. How do you like London?
    - ☐ a) I do appreciate it.
    - ☐ b) Thank you very much.
    - ☐ c) Quite.
    - ☐ d) Very much indeed.

13. Will you take the 12.00 train to Birmingham?
    - ☐ a) Oh yes, I do.
    - ☐ b) I'll make it.
    - ☐ c) I hope so.
    - ☐ d) Yes, I will.

14. Thank you very much for all your help.
    - ☐ a) Don't mention it.
    - ☐ b) Please.
    - ☐ c) I meant well.
    - ☐ d) Never mind.

15. Will you be able to fly to New York next week?
    - ☐ a) No, I can't.
    - ☐ b) I think.
    - ☐ c) No, I won't.
    - ☐ d) I believe.

16. Have the passengers gone through the customs yet?
    - ☐ a) I think.
    - ☐ b) I don't think it.
    - ☐ c) I don't think.
    - ☐ d) I don't think so.

17. Will we be too late?
    - ☐ a) I don't hope so.
    - ☐ b) Let's hope.
    - ☐ c) Let's hope not.
    - ☐ d) Don't hope.

18. She won't like it, will she?
    - ☐ a) I suppose not.
    - ☐ b) I don't suppose.
    - ☐ c) I don't suppose it.
    - ☐ d) Don't suppose.

19. Will she come to the party?
    - ☐ a) I hope it.
    - ☐ b) I hope so.
    - ☐ c) I don't hope.
    - ☐ d) I will not hope so.

20. Has the plane arrived yet?
    - ☐ a) I don't know.
    - ☐ b) I know not.
    - ☐ c) I don't know it.
    - ☐ d) I know it not.

Revision Exercises III

1. Use 'all, both, half', etc.

Example: He spent *his time* in pubs and on race-courses. (half)
He spent *half his time* in pubs and on race-courses.

1. The office building was *a mile* from their house. (half) 2. *Their money* was spent on household machines. (all) 3. They offered *a big sum* to those willing to leave the docks. (quite) 4. It was *a pity* that you couldn't go to the party. (such) 5. *His sons* attended a comprehensive school. (both) 6. *The sum* was not enough for the workers. (double) 7. She was *a pretty girl.* (quite)

2. Answer the questions

Example: Is this your house? Yes, ... (No, ...)
Yes, *it's mine.* (No, it isn't mine.)

1. Does this car belong to him? Yes, it's ... 2. Is this our room? No, ... 3. Are these their books? No, ... 4. Is this your wallet? Yes, ... 5. Is this her seat? No, ... 6. Does this garden belong to them? Yes, ...

3. Connect the sentences by using 'if'

Example: Don't drive on the right. You'll soon land in hospital.
If you drive on the right, *you'll* soon land in hospital.

1. Don't walk on the inside of the pavement when out with a lady. She won't like it. 2. Don't shake hands when meeting people. They'll find it unusual. 3. Don't remain seated when a lady leaves your table. She'll be surprised. 4. Don't forget to leave a tip for the waiter. He won't be very pleased. 5. Don't refuse to pay for a round of drinks when in company. People won't ask you again. 6. Don't drink when driving a car. You may lose your driving-licence.

4. Shorten the sentences by using participles

Example: The letter *which introduced* Mr Nuttle had been written by his sister.
The letter *introducing* Mr Nuttle had been written by his sister.

III

1. Bilk, who still lay in his hospital bed, was arrested for attempted murder. 2. Bilk crept into his wife's bedroom with a bottle that contained poison. 3. His wife, who was asleep, didn't hear him enter the house. 4. The operation, which took place in the morning, was Bilk's alibi. 5. The inspector who made inquiries found no proof at first. 6. The dog, which was accustomed to following its master, went straight to the hospital.

5. Use prepositions to connect the sentences

Example: (after) Mrs Parks waited for five minutes. Then she saw the bus coming.
After waiting for five minutes, Mrs Parks saw the bus coming.

1. (after) Mrs Parks sat down. Then she heard the bus driver tell her to get up. 2. (without) The bus driver did not say a word. He fetched a policeman. 3. (in spite of) Mrs Parks was in the right. She was arrested. 4. (before) The Negro leaders called a bus boycott. They held a meeting. 5. (instead of) The Negroes didn't take the buses on Monday morning. They walked or got a lift. 6. (without) Mrs Parks didn't want to make trouble. But she started the movement for freedom.

6. Use the gerund

Example: Do you mind *if I smoke?*
Do you mind *my (me) smoking?*

1. Do you mind if I open the window? 2. Do you mind if she uses your phone? 3. Do you mind if I turn on the radio? 4. Does your mother mind if we go now? 5. Does your father mind if they go to the theatre together? 6. Do you mind if he asks your sister for a dance?

7. since or for?

1. We have suffered ... years. 2. ... 1955 many things have improved. 3. ... we were born we've never known the meaning of happiness. 4. The buses have been boycotted ... last Monday. 5. We've been treated badly ... a long time. 6. ... many years we've been kicked about.

8. Past tense or present perfect?

Example: A tunnel under the Channel/to be dreamt of/for nearly two centuries.
A tunnel under the Channel *has been* dreamt of for nearly two centuries.
It/to be started/in 1880.
It *was* started in 1880.

1. An agreement between the British and the French/to be signed/some years ago 2. Since gas/to be found/in the North Sea during the sixties, Britain/to become/ self-supporting *(selbstversorgend)* as far as gas is concerned 3. Britain/to look for/ North Sea oil for several years 4. The production of North Sea oil/to give/fresh hope to Britain 5. Britain/to be/a member of the European Community since 1972 6. The Empire/to reach/the height of its power in 1902 7. Up to now the Commonwealth/not to be/a great success

9. Short answers with 'so' and 'neither (nor)'

Example: I saw the Tower. *So did* my brother.
I couldn't drive on the left. *Nor could* my wife.

1. I disliked going by Underground. (friend) 2. I preferred riding on the top of a bus. (aunt) 3. I wouldn't drive my own car through London. (sister) 4. I would take a taxi instead. (grandmother) 5. The young Frenchman wanted the company of young people. (Ingrid) 6. I haven't been to the theatre yet. (sister) 7. My sister loves London. (I) 8. The English drink a lot of tea. (Irish)

10. Use the passive voice

Leave out the by-agent whenever possible
Example: We'll have to deal with *this problem.*
This problem will have *to be dealt with.*

1. We'll have to pay for *our seats.* 2. People look upon *the Empire* as a thing of the past *(Vergangenheit).* 3. People speak of *Shakespeare* as the world's greatest dramatist. 4. We cannot depend on his *promises.* 5. The British took *Gibraltar* in 1704. (by) 6. The world must take care of *the developing nations.*

11. in order to

Example: The oil companies have insured themselves. Thus they will be covered against accidents.
In order to be covered against accidents the oil companies have insured themselves.

1. Britain will use her North Sea oil. Thus she will become independent of the Middle East. 2. The steel rigs are firmly fastened to the sea-bed. Thus they are protected against storms and waves. 3. Industrial countries need more and more energy. Thus they increase their production. 4. Britain also uses coal, gas and atomic energy. Thus she makes her oil reserves last longer. 5. Britain has invited foreign companies to look for North Sea oil. Thus she avoids spending her own money. 6. Europe must increase its production. Thus it will avoid unemployment.

12. Use the infinitive

Example: We need a car in which we can get home easily.
We need a car *to get home in* easily.

1. Britain was the first country that changed an Empire into a Commonwealth. 2. I hope we'll find a good hotel in which we can spend the night. 3. Shakespeare was not the only poet that understood the human heart. 4. John Smith was not the first person who placed slow sellers in good positions. 5. We wanted an assistant who could help us. 6. The best thing we can do is to learn English well.

13. one – ones

Example: Our armchair is getting old. We must buy (new)
We must buy *a new one.*

1. This car is too expensive. We must buy (cheaper) 2. Don't read boring books. Read (entertaining) 3. This newspaper is too political. I'd like (non-political) 4. She always wears last year's dresses. She should wear (modern) 5. No, I didn't like his articles. I've read (better) 6. I must tell you some jokes, some (good)